BIBLICAL WISDOM FOR A MAXIMUM MARRIAGE

A TOPICAL STUDY OF PROVERBS FOR COUPLES

DENNIS R. DAVIDSON

Biblical Wisdom for a Maximum Marriage

Cover design and book layout by Dennis R. Davidson

ACKNOWLEDGMENTS

I have nothing but the utmost appreciation of my gifted bride, Connie, for her devoted willingness in proofreading and editing this publication. Her proficiency makes sentences more readable and enjoyable. I treasure her common sense and expressed suggestions on how to get my thoughts aligned for easier reading. In addition, I am continually awed by her enthusiasm to want to help couples achieve godly marriages.

Marriage wisdom is enriched from experienced mentors. I thank Dewey Wilson, Ph.D., and his wife, Lynne, for their continued support of mentoring couples and through the resources from their ministry, Strong Marriages.

I thank my pastor and friend, Kris Segrest, for his spiritual insights and inspiration through his remarkable messages each week. I am always impressed with his mastery of showing me how to enthusiastically apply God's wisdom in my everyday life.

I will always be grateful to have known for just a short while my dear late friend, Jeff Lauer. He encouraged me beyond what I thought I could ever achieve with my own limited thinking. He was the spark that launched me into writing this book as well as my previous devotionals for men, *Minutes in His Presence*. He was truly a gift from God and will be sorely missed until I see him again in eternity.

CONTENTS

A Maximum Marriage
GROWS SPIRITUALLY

A Maximum Marriage
PRAYS TOGETHER

A Maximum Marriage
ACQUIRES WISDOM

A Maximum Marriage
COMMUNICATES WITH GRACE

HOW TO USE THIS STUDY

Seeking a maximum marriage should be the desire of every married couple. Allow me to define what I mean by a "maximum marriage." I am not implying that the relationship has maxed out or has been perfected. No perfect marriage exists because we are all imperfect. No matter what condition your marriage is currently in, achieving a greater, higher, utmost relationship *to the fullest* is my hope for you and your spouse.

A study of the wisdom handed down to us from Solomon is a great resource for developing our utmost embodiment of the marriage institution designed by God. The purpose of Proverbs is explained in the first six verses.

> 1 These are the proverbs of Solomon, David's son, king of Israel.
> 2 Their purpose is to teach people wisdom and discipline, to help them understand the insights of the wise.
> 3 Their purpose is to teach people to live disciplined and successful lives, to help them do what is right just, and fair.
> 4 These proverbs will give insight to the simple, knowledge and discernment to the young.
> 5 Let the wise listen to these proverbs and become even wiser.
> Let those with understanding receive guidance
> 6 by exploring the meaning in these proverbs and parables, the words of the wise and their riddles.

The book of Proverbs not only teaches how to think, but also how to do "what is right, just, and fair." These scriptures convey how to align with God's design for every aspect of life, especially the marriage relationship. I hope to show when you apply God's wisdom, you can build a successful marriage with maximum benefits. The principles found in Proverbs should be the foundation for husbands and wives as they face life's most challenging difficulties.

You may choose to read this book straight through by reading one devotional per day. Or you may choose to delve into a particular section that you're coping with at the moment and read individual devotions related to that subject. I have divided the book into sectional topics that are relative to everyday marital matters.

You'll notice two boxes to the left of each heading. If you and your spouse are reading this book together, each of you may check off a box when you have completed the devotional for that day. I suggest that you each have your own colored highlighter so that you can highlight particular sentences that stand out to you individually. Then you can color your "completion" box in your appropriate color.

I believe it's not enough to just read this book and be on your way. Therefore, I have added applications at the end of each devotion: "Take Action" and "Pray." Making an effort to achieve the maximum marriage must be continually applied. It doesn't happen by itself.

The "Take Action" items can be done together or individually. If you are the only one in your relationship reading this book, persist in the activities by yourself and perhaps your mate will take notice.

I have suggested prayer topics to assist you in praying together as a couple. Our Heavenly Father loves to hear his children speak in their own words (See pages 30–35 for more about praying together). The Lord blesses the couple that prays together.

God has much to teach us, and I can't wait to take this learning journey with you — so, let's begin!

— *Dennis R. Davidson*

FEARING GOD FOR WISDOM

Fear of the LORD is the foundation of true knowledge, but fools despise wisdom and discipline.

— Proverbs 1:7 (See also Proverbs 9:10)

Solomon starts out acknowledging the most important facet of a Christian life is fear of the Lord. It's the beginning of knowledge. Therefore, the most important facet of building a strong marriage is a couple who seeks and fears God.

What is fear of the Lord? It doesn't mean being afraid of God, since we know God is our Father who always loves and forgives us. It is a joyful awareness of God's magnificence and a grateful realization that only in Him do our hearts find true peace. This is not a fear that leads to despair because of our sinfulness, but it is to be combined with trust and love. As C. S. Lewis describes it, having a fear of the Lord is being filled with awe, in which you "feel wonder and a certain shrinking" or "a sense of inadequacy to cope with such a supernatural" God. It is a reference and respect that comes forth out of love for the Lord.

Here are some good, basic descriptions of what "fear of the Lord" is really all about:

- An awe-inspiring reverence.
- Personal awareness of the awesome and majestic sovereignty of God.
- Seeking holiness to glorify Him.
- A feeling of reverence, awe, respect, and adoration toward the Almighty.

A proper fear of the Lord can lead to the following blessings:

- Life
- Happiness
- Satisfaction
- Strong confidence

- Prolong your days on this earth
- Your children will have security
- Wealth, riches, honor and prosperity
- Dwell in safety

This second list seems to come from a *New York Times* best-seller book on achieving a successful life. But these qualities come straight from Scripture about fearing the Lord. Read the list again as it would pertain to your marriage. Certainly, you would want these blessings in your relationship.

In order to have a maximum marriage, you both need a fear of the Lord. Look at this diagram. As each of you pursue God (fearing Him) and get closer to Him, you get closer to each other. As you spend time in His Word, in prayer, and loving Him, His characteristics will overflow onto you. For instance, you'll become more loving, more patient, more accepting (mercy), and more forgiving. As these characteristics overflow on you individually, they will then overflow on to your spouse from you.

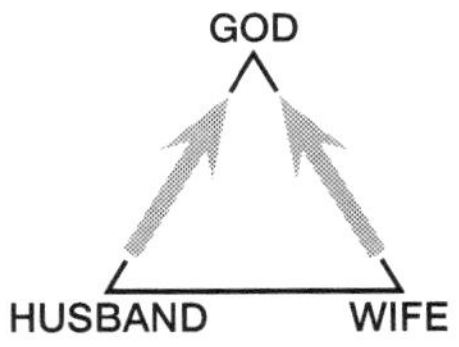

Fear God and keep His commandments, for this is the whole duty of man.
— Ecclesiastes 12:13

TAKE ACTION

- Make a daily, appointed time to spend with the Lord, either together or individually, reading His Word and praying.

PRAY

Him:
- Pray for your wife's wisdom to increase.
- Thank God for your wife and your marriage.

Her:
- Ask God to give your husband wisdom to become strong in his daily decision making — at his work and in the home.
- Thank God for your husband and his intelligence.

SEEKING GOOD COUNSEL

Plans fail for lack of counsel, but with many advisors they succeed.
— Proverbs 15:22

A successful husband and wife pursue God, seek God, and desire to know His ways for every plan they make in their relationship. If you had premarital counseling before your wedding day, that's great. But for the years afterward, you shouldn't leave it up to yourselves to come up with hopeful strategies.

Why not have an experienced Christian couple who have been through the ups and downs of married life help you make wise choices? This "mentor" couple would be like a teacher, a coach or tutor who could show you the ropes. Even the best athletes in the world have coaches to help them improve their game.

If your church does not have a marriage mentoring program, go online to **StrongMarriages.com** and order their mentoring materials. Then seek out a couple whom you admire spiritually and have them go through the materials with you. More than likely, they would be honored that you asked them, but might also think they are ill-equipped to instruct you. If each of you go through the materials from Strong Marriages together, each of you will grow and be blessed.

Stephen and Alex Kendrick describe a powerful reason to have mentors in their book, *The Love Dare*:

> "Mighty sequoia trees tower hundreds of feet in the air and can withstand intense environmental pressures. Lightning can strike them, fierce winds can blow, and forest fires can rage around them. But the sequoia endures, standing firm, only growing stronger through the trials.
>
> "One of the secrets to the strength of this giant tree is what goes on below the surface. Unlike many trees, they reach out and interlock their roots with the sequoias around them. Each becomes empowered and reinforced by the strength of the others.
>
> "...[Couples] who interlock their lives in a network of other strong marriages radically increase their chances of surviving the fiercest of storms."*

Mentors encourage and cheer you on when otherwise you might want to give up. They can assist you in making wise decisions or warn you if you're about to make a bad decision. Research shows that couples who have marriage mentors are happier and healthier.

Even if your marriage is fairly stable, you could still use a godly mentor couple to encourage you and challenge you. Every marriage can improve and be more successful with counsel as Solomon says. If your marriage is in serious trouble and mentors don't seem to be qualified, then seek professional counseling. Seeking help is not a sign of weakness, it a sign of wise strength. Your marriage is worth fighting for and always worth the effort.

A wise man will hear and increase learning, and a man of understanding will attain wise counsel.
— Proverbs 1:5 (NKJV)

The way of a fool is right in his own eyes, but a wise man is he who listens to counsel.
— Proverbs 12:15

TAKE ACTION

- Don't be afraid of partnering with a mentor couple. The benefits far outweigh the awkwardness you think you might encounter.
- Actively seek a mentoring program, a personal mentor couple, or professional counseling.
- Consider starting a marriage mentoring program in your church.

PRAY

Him: • Ask God to give you the courage to look for a mentor couple. If you pray believing a couple is there for you, God will bring them to you.

Her: • Ask God for understanding in the need for mentors.

**The Love Dare*, Copyright © 2008 by Stephen & Alex Kendrick. B & H Publishing Group, Nashville, TN

☐☐ FEARING GOD AND HATING WHAT HE HATES, Part 1

All who fear the L*ORD* *will hate evil. Therefore, I hate pride and arrogance, corruption and perverse speech.*

— Proverbs 8:13

Notice this Proverb starts out with "All." It's a small word that means much. It means each, everyone, every single person. If you really fear the Lord, if you are in complete awe of His Sovereignty, then you will hate all manner of evil.

Those who have saturated themselves with the attributes of God, will then hate what goes against His holiness. But we like to portray Him as a God of love. Does He, can He, truly *hate*? This verse certainly says so. He gives us particular examples here of things He hates — pride, arrogance, corruption, and perverted speech. A maximum marriage would want to get rid of these destructive forces at all costs.

We'll look at the first two today and the others tomorrow.

PRIDE — This is where all sin originates. It's the main cause of divorces. C. S. Lewis said, "A proud man is always looking down on things and people; and, of course, as long as you are looking down, you cannot see something that is above you." Pride does not like the sovereignty of God. Not totally believing in the sovereign rights of God to manage the details of your life, or marriage, is nothing but selfish pride.

When pride comes, then comes disgrace, but with humility comes wisdom.

— Proverbs 11:2

Everyone proud in heart is an abomination to the L*ORD*…

— Proverbs 16:5 (NKJV)

Pride goes before destruction, and a haughty spirit before a fall.

— Proverbs 16:18 (ESV)

ARROGANCE — This may be our most difficult quality to acknowledge. It's our pompous ego. It says "I am important" and "I am more important than others." An arrogant person believes he is always right. No one likes being around an arrogant person. It's because they dictate the conversation, and it's all about them. Not too long ago I realized I was arrogant. That hit hard. No wonder I had difficulty making friends. No wonder my wife had difficulty speaking to me.

The way to battle this arrogance is to yield to the sovereignty of God in all the details of your life, and to be fully committed to Him. Serve your spouse's needs over your own. Personally, I never realized how unhappy I was being arrogant. When I concentrated on serving my wife first, peaceful contentment fulfilled me in ways I had never known.

The proud and arrogant person — "Mocker" is his name — behaves with insolent fury.

— Proverbs 21:24 (NIV)

Live in harmony with one another. Do not be haughty, but associate with the lowly. Never be wise in your own sight.

— Romans 12:16 (ESV)

TAKE ACTION

- Take a hard look at where you personally may have too much pride or arrogance in yourself.

PRAY

Him: • Ask God to help you destroy pride in your life.

Her: • Ask God to give you a desire to serve your husband with contentment.

FEARING GOD AND HATING WHAT HE HATES, Part 2

All who fear the Lord *will hate evil. Therefore, I hate pride and arrogance, corruption and perverse speech.*

— Proverbs 8:13

The concluding items in this verse that the Lord hates are corruption and perverse speech.

CORRUPTION — We easily recognize evil ways: murder; adultery; stealing; lying; deception. So it's probably safe to say we hate people who do those things. But I want to challenge you to look inward, and to see what Jesus says about these qualities. In Matthew 5 He associates murder with just being angry at another, "If you are even angry with someone, you are subject to judgment!" Later in the same chapter He compares adultery with lust. He essentially says if you even look at another with lust, you've committed adultery in your heart.

What about stealing? You might say, "Well, I don't take from others." But Paul says in 1 Corinthians 7 you shouldn't deprive yourself to your spouse. You gave up the rights to yourself when you married. Denying your spouse's needs is stealing from them.

Have you ever lied to your spouse? Have you ever deceived them just to get something for yourself? Ouch! But remember your old self has passed away and now you are a new creation in Jesus Christ (2 Cor. 5:17) with new desires to obey God and a new passion to serve Him. Our attitudes can be transformed by the Spirit.

Throw off your old sinful nature and your former way of life, which is corrupted by lust and deception. Instead, let the Spirit renew your thoughts and attitudes.

— Ephesians 4:22–23

PERVERSE SPEECH — Your mouth was created to praise God, encourage each other, and speak truth. Perverse speech occurs when you use your words for evil purposes such as cursing, gossiping, using foul language, and lying. Ephesians 4:29 says, "Don't use foul or abusive language. Let everything you say be good and helpful, so that your words will be an encouragement to those who hear them." In Matthew 15:11, Jesus indicates that perversion is a matter of the heart: "What goes into someone's mouth does not defile them, but what comes out of their mouth, that is what defiles them" (NIV).

Let your speech always be gracious, seasoned with salt, so that you may know how you ought to answer each person.
— Colossians 4:6 (ESV)

The remedy for all these evils is an unwavering faith in God's sovereign grace. God's Word is very clear. You are supposed to hate the things that our Almighty God hates. To achieve true freedom and joy in a maximum marriage, you must not practice those things God hates. Instead practice kindness, faithfulness, purity, and encouraging words.

TAKE ACTION

- Make a stand today that you are going to put away all manner of evils as indicated in this Proverb. Ask your spouse to be watchful when these wrongs flair up and to be a supportive, loving, forgiving and gracious person to you when you fail.

PRAY

Him:
- Petition God to create within you a hate for the things He hates.
- Ask God to give you an attitude of grace at all times.

Her:
- Ask God to give you a character of kindness, love, and grace.
- Ask God to build your marriage in a way that would portray the loving and peaceful environment that He desires.

FINDING FAVOR FROM THE LORD

The man who finds a wife finds a treasure, and he receives favor from the L*ORD.*

— Proverbs 18:22

At first glance, this verse may seem to be all about men. But it's for both the man and the woman.

A WIFE — This is referring to a woman that is worthy to be called by such an honorable name. A wife is esteemed. This wife is a jewel of great value. The title of "wife" means she takes care of her role in the partnership.

Who can find a virtuous and capable wife? She is more precious than rubies. Her husband can trust her, and she will greatly enrich his life.

— Proverbs 31:10–11

A treasure (or some translations use "A good thing") — In order to meet this qualification, the woman has to first meet the criteria of a "wife." That means you should have your stuff together. Proverbs 31:12 states, "She brings him *good* all the days of his life." The Hebrew goes on to infer that the only way a man can give his full mental capacity of love to a woman is if she has the ability to respond to his love. Women are designed by God to be the responders to a man's love. So "a good thing" is a woman who is capable of receiving from the ultimate source of a man's soul — his love — and responding in kind.

Receives favor from the LORD — This is one of those "if-then" verses. *If* all the criteria are met in the first phrase of the verse, *then* you will receive blessings. Do you want God's blessings on your marriage? The recipe is this: A man loving his wife with his entire soul and a wife loving him in return by being virtuous.

Your spouse is a treasure. Think about what you treasure materially. Is it your house? Is it your car? Would you treat something that you treasure harshly? What if you were gifted with a Stradivarius violin (worth millions) or a rare and priceless Testore cello? Max Lucado was loaned a Testore cello once for a sermon illustration:

> "Wanting to illustrate the fragile sanctity of marriage, I asked the owner to place the nearly-three-centuries-old relic on the stage, and I explained its worth to the church.
>
> "How do you think I treated the relic? Did I twirl it, flip it, or pluck the strings? No way. The cello was far too valuable for my clumsy fingers. Besides, its owner loaned it to me. I dared not dishonor his treasure.
>
> "On your wedding day, God loaned you His work of art: an intricately crafted, precisely formed masterpiece. He entrusted you with a one-of-a-kind creation. Value her. Honor him. Make your wife the object of your highest devotion. Make your husband the recipient of your deepest passion. Love the one who wears your ring."*

Your spouse is an exquisite gift from God. By respecting each other's value, you have the power to unlock maximum potential in each other and then receive a huge blessing.

Let each one of you in particular so love his own wife as himself, and let the wife see that she respects her husband.

— Ephesians 5:33 (NKJV)

TAKE ACTION

- Give each other a little gift today that says, "I value you."
- Start saying "please" and "thank you" more often.

PRAY

Him:

- Thank God for loaning you His masterpiece in your wife.
- Ask Him to give you good judgment in always treasuring her.

Her:

- Thank God for the gift of your husband.
- Ask Him to give you the ability to respect and respond to his love.

---

* *Facing Your Giants,* Copyright ©2006 by Max Lucado, Thomas Nelson, Inc., Nashville, TN

TRUSTING THE LORD

Trust in the LORD *with all your heart, and do not lean on your own understanding. In all your ways acknowledge Him, and He will make straight your paths.*

— Proverbs 3:5–6 (ESV)

There is a purpose for your marriage. God brought both of you together to seek His will for your lives. Isaiah 58:11 says, "The LORD will guide you continually…." In Ephesians 2:10 Paul says you are God's masterpiece and you can do the good things he has planned for you. Psalm 37:23 states, "The LORD directs the steps of the godly. He delights in every detail of their lives." God's promises are true! So how can you find God's way and purpose in your marriage?

1. Have a trusting confidence. In order to put your complete confidence in someone, you must love them. To love someone is to know that person. You must desire to know God better in order to love Him more, and then you'll be able to trust Him.

You are not to depend on your own understanding. Solomon *does* tell us to seek understanding throughout Proverbs. But it's God's wisdom we are to seek, not our own. I would much rather put my trust in the Creator of my life rather than trusting my own tendencies.

Be not wise in your own eyes; fear the LORD, *and turn away from evil. It will be healing to your flesh and refreshment to your bones.*

— Proverbs 3:7–8 (ESV)

2. Have a total commitment. Spending time with God will allow you to trust with *all* your heart. Giving Him your *all* will give you a complete confidence that He'll do what He says He's going to do. Acknowledge God as your sovereign Lord over *everything* in your life.

Commit to the LORD *whatever you do, and He will establish your plans."*

— Proverbs 16:3 (NIV)

3. Enjoy the thrilling consequence. He *will* show you the divine direction in your life (and marriage) three ways:

- He'll speak to you through His Word. Psalm 119:105 says, "Your Word is a lamp to guide my feet and a light for my path."
- He'll show you through prayer. By spending time in prayer, God will speak to your Spirit. You just have to listen.
- He'll show you by His wisdom. Adrian Rogers defined God's wisdom as "sanctified common sense." You just have to seek His understanding by studying His Word and spending time with Him.

The New King James Version of verse 6 says, "He shall direct your paths." The Hebrew for the word "direct" means to cut a path, to clear the way, to make smooth. There is no doubt that in your life there will be valleys and storms. But God will make a way. He will bulldoze the way.

A maximum marriage is a trusting God marriage. Acknowledging Him in the center of your union will make the journey smoother and straighter. He promises it.

TAKE ACTION

- Discuss with each other if there are any areas of your marriage which are not totally committed to God.
- Commit to spend more time with God together.

PRAY

Him:
- Praise God for His promise of making your pathway smooth.
- Ask Him to give you direction and "sanctified common sense" in every area of your life.

Her:
- Praise God for making you His masterpiece.
- Commit to Him every area of your marriage relationship.

BOOSTING YOUR POTENTIAL, Part 1

Above all else, guard your heart, for everything you do flows from it.
— Proverbs 4:23 (NIV)

Chances are you own a car. You know you're not supposed to put sand in the gas tank. If you do, the car will sputter and die. On the other hand, if you put high octane or super unleaded fuel in the tank, it'll run even better. Your love for your spouse flows from your heart. So it is essential to fill it up with God's high powered love.

Guard it.

What you put into your heart will come out. Your heart is your essence — the deepest part of what is truly you. It's the center from which your dreams, desires, passions, motives, thoughts, emotions, decisions, and actions arise. So it's no wonder that Solomon says to guard it!

Have you noticed that if something is important, you guard it? If you have a wallet, you don't leave it out where anyone can take it. When you leave your car or house, you lock it up. We spend a lot of effort each day keeping ourselves safe. The same effort should be applied to your heart.

Everything you do.

Watch what you take into your mind. What you read and see over and over again will eventually make it's way into your spiritual and emotional heart. Studying the Bible on a regular basis will implant God's truths into your inner identity.

Two statements later in this chapter, Solomon advises his son to "Look straight ahead, and fix your eyes on what lies before you" (Prov. 4:25). What you see and do goes straight to your heart. Everything. Feed the heart ungodly entertainment, and you get a soiled heart. Feed your eyes on what is pure and you get a godly heart.

Flows.

Your words, your thoughts, your choices, your decisions, your priorities — all come from your heart. When a heart is full of God's love, beautiful words and ideas flow from it. You need to protect your heart against bitterness, impatience, greed, jealousy, idolatry, and anger. These traits will overtake your heart if you let them. You must also guard your heart against unsafe people, unhealthy relationships, and ungodly activities. The NLT version interprets the last phrase of this Proverb this way: "it determines the course of your life." The New King James Version says, "...for out of it *springs* the issues of life" [Emphasis mine].

Protect your heart so that positive words, ideas, and actions flow from it, or *spring* from it, for the good of your relationship. Be on guard! Filling up with godly additives boosts your potential to achieve the maximum marriage.

Be on guard. Stand firm in the faith. Be courageous. Be strong. And do everything with love.
— 1 Corinthians 16:13–14

TAKE ACTION

- Take a hard look at how you can boost your input of spiritual things.
- Dig deep into your inner heart and tell each other specifically what you love about each other.

PRAY

Him:
- Ask God to put a shield around your heart to protect it from the enemy's fiery darts.
- Ask God to create a clean heart in you just as He did for David (Psalm 51:10).

Her:
- Ask God to purify your heart and mind with His holiness.
- Pray Psalm 26:2.

☐☐ BOOSTING YOUR POTENTIAL, Part 2

Above all else, guard your heart, for everything you do flows from it.
— Proverbs 4:23 (NIV)

You face a battle every day — a battle for your heart. Solomon says to make it a priority "above all else" and put a shield around your heart.

When speaking of "your heart," the reference is to your mind. The warning here is to guard your thoughts. Zig Ziglar put it this way, "Get rid of stinkin' thinkin'." Do not allow your mind to become polluted. Trash in becomes trash out. For a peaceful, maximum marriage, keep your mind focused on good things.

As Paul tells us in Philippians 4:8, "Fix your thoughts on what is true, and honorable, and right, and pure, and lovely, and admirable. Think about things that are excellent and worthy of praise."

The mind reflects who you really are. What you say and do is a reflection of what is in your mind. What's in your mind determines your attitude and your action in all circumstances. Therefore you must be very careful about what you allow your mind to receive.

For where your treasure is, there your heart will be also.
— Luke 12:24

A great way to guard your mind is to put on the full armor of God (See Ephesians 6:10–18). Notice how a breastplate protects the heart. And a helmet protects the mind. The shield strengthens our faith. There are five defensive protectors mentioned and two offensive weapons. The sword refers to the Bible. You must saturate your mind with scripture. And most importantly, prayer will be your strongest weapon.

Put on all of God's armor so that you will be able to stand firm against all strategies of the devil.

— Ephesians 6:11

Realize the treasure that God has given you by what is known as the mind. Fill it with daily scripture. Fill it with good thoughts. Force yourself to say positive things in all circumstances.

Wrong thinking not only produces wrong words and wrong actions, but this kind of thinking also hinders your spiritual growth. When you guard your heart with diligence and work the plans of your lives according to God's pathway in the Bible, you will then be putting yourselves in a position to receive all that God has for you in your marriage.

TAKE ACTION

- Read Ephesians 6:10–18 about putting on the whole armor of God.
- Encourage one another to say more positive things throughout the day and less of the negatives.
- Tell your spouse three things that you admire about them. Better yet, put it on a sticky note and give it to them.

PRAY

Him:
- Pray Psalm 51:10 and ask God to create a new heart within you and to fill your mind with pure thoughts.
- Express to God how ecstatic you are about her.

Her:
- Pray Philippians 4:8 and ask God to always fix your thoughts on things that are excellent and worthy of praise.

PURSUING THE GODLY LIFE, Part 1

Whoever pursues righteousness and unfailing love will find life, righteousness, and honor.

— Proverbs 21:21

In the New King James Version of the Bible, there are 67 references to the word "righteous," and 88 references to the word "righteousness." Therefore, it would be good to understand what it is in order to be able to pursue it.

It is most often translated to mean "justice," or "divine holiness." Pursuing righteousness is pursuing the character of Christ and desiring holiness more than fleshly indulgence. You will avoid the temptation to become self-righteous when you understand that true righteousness begins with godly humility. Pride and self-righteousness cannot remain in the presence of a holy God. Pursuing righteousness begins when a humble heart seeks the continual presence of God. To be righteous is to be right with God and acceptable to Him.

There are many instances in the Bible that support what Solomon conveys here in pursuing righteousness. Christ says in Matthew 5:6 (NKJV), "Blessed are those who hunger and thirst for righteousness, for they shall be filled." And in Matthew 6:33 (ESV), "Seek first the kingdom of God and his righteousness, and all these things will be added to you."

The second item Solomon mentions to pursue is unfailing love. The word used here has been translated many different ways: loyalty, kindness, mercy (lovingkindness, grace). Most often it is translated "mercy." This quality of God is one that God requires of you. It denotes compassion and love, not just feelings or emotions, expressed in tangible ways. Showing compassion and merciful action to your spouse are the essence of a spiritual life and experiencing a maximum marriage.

The result? You'll find life, righteousness, and honor. "Life" indicates happiness, contentment and fulfillment. Isn't that what you desire? Then, you'll find righteousness. Of course that seems logical. If you pursue righteousness, you'll find it. The NIV uses "prosperity" meaning success and flourishing. Commentators tend to think that this second reference to "righteousness" refers to the rewards of righteousness which can be prosperity. Then you'll also find honor, which is honesty, fairness, or integrity in your beliefs and actions.

The maximum marriage is where both husband and wife are pursuing, on an individual basis, holiness and kindness, resulting in obtaining happiness, fulfillment, and prosperity. When you focus on pleasing God, loving your spouse becomes easier. You both become content knowing the heavenly Father cares for you and will give you all your needs.

The righteous flourish and prosperity abound till the moon is no more.
— Psalm 72:7 (NIV)

TAKE ACTION

- Discuss how you both can hunger and thirst more for righteousness.
- Talk about areas in your lifestyle that may not necessarily be righteous — such as TV shows you watch or friends that might be a bad influence.

PRAY

Him:
- Ask God to give you contentment in your marriage.
- Ask Him to show you how you can show your wife more mercy.

Her:
- Ask God to give you a drive to become righteous, but not self-righteous.
- Thank God for your prosperous life.

PURSUING THE GODLY LIFE, Part 2

Choose a good reputation over great riches; being held in high esteem is better than silver or gold.

— Proverbs 22:1

There are many things you can pursue in life. You can pursue being in good physical shape. You can pursue making yourself look attractive. You can pursue climbing the corporate ladder towards a successful career and high income. You can also live for whatever gives you pleasure.

In these few words, Solomon tells us what to pursue over great riches. Integrity. "A good name earned by honorable behavior, godly wisdom, moral courage, and personal integrity is more desirable than great riches" (Prov. 22:1 AMP). This does not mean that your purpose is to put yourself first. Your purpose is to revere God in who you are and what you do.

Observe how Rick Warren puts it in *The Purpose Driven Life*:

> "It's not about you. The purpose of your life is far greater than your own personal fulfillment, your peace of mind, or even your happiness. It's far greater than your family, your career, or even your wildest dreams and ambitions. If you want to know why you were placed on this planet, you must begin with God. You were born *by* His purpose and *for* His purpose."*

Your life's goal should be to honor God, give honest work, have personal integrity, and have a good testimony for others to see. Focusing on yourself will never reveal your life's purpose. You were made by God and for God — and until you understand that, life will never make sense.

It's in Christ that we find out who we are and what we are living for. Long before we first heard of Christ... he had his eye on us, had

**The Purpose Driven Life,* Copyright © 2002 by Rick Warren, Zondervan, Grand Rapids, Michigan.

designs on us for glorious living, part of the overall purpose he is working out in everything and everyone.

— Ephesians 1:11 (MSG)

Now let's turn this toward the purpose of your marriage. Since everything you do is for God's purpose, then everything that happens in your marriage relationship should center around God. Knowing this purpose gives meaning to your marriage, simplifies your marriage, focuses your marriage, and drives your marriage. Marriage is not meant to be hard. Your pursuit together is to be towards holiness, not your own personal happiness. Knowing this is far better than even money.

If you pursue "things" to satisfy you, you'll never be satisfied. If you want a life free from worry, anxiety, and fear, then pursue a godly life before everything else. Seek God first, and He will take care of you.

A life devoted to things is a dead life, a stump; a God-shaped life is a flourishing tree.

— Proverbs 11:28 (MSG)

TAKE ACTION

- Read Jeremiah 17:7–8 and make it your goal to live a life of honoring God in all you do, so that your marriage will be a flourishing tree.

PRAY

Him:

- Thank God that He had His eye on you long before you became His child.
- Ask God to give you complete trust in Him in all areas of your life.

Her:

- Thank God for giving you a purpose in life.
- Praise God for His goodness to free you from worry, anxiety, and fear.

TUNING INTO GOD

[1]Listen to what I say, and treasure my commands. [2]Tune your ears to wisdom, and concentrate on understanding. [3]Cry out for insight, and ask for understanding.

— Proverbs 2:1–3

Dennis Rainey says, "Praying together may be the single most important spiritual discipline you and your spouse will ever share."[1] Perhaps you could even complete the following phrase before you read it entirely: The family that prays together, stays together. A 1991 Research Poll backs this up — that when couples pray together, divorce rates plummet to less than 1 percent![2] And this is not just praying before meals (which is appropriate), but at other times as well.

Jesus said in Matthew 18:19–20, "If two of you agree here on earth concerning anything you ask, my Father in heaven will do it for you. For where two or three gather together as my followers, I am there among them." That should be powerful motivation to seek God's wisdom by praying as two! The sincere agreement of two people in prayer is more powerful than the superficial agreement of thousands, because the Holy Spirit is with them.

Pray in the Spirit at all times, and on every occasion. Stay alert and be persistent in your prayers for all believers everywhere.

— Ephesians 6:18

In this Proverb, Solomon speaks of the discipline of prayer. It consists of reading His Word (verse 1), and an inner desire (verse 2) for the pursuit of wisdom. James 1:5 repeats this point, "If you need

1. *Two Hearts Praying As One,* Dennis & Barbara Rainey ©2002, Multnomah Books, Colorado Springs, CO
2. Commissioned Research entitled "Evangelical Christians," Gallup Research Corporation Summary Report, May, 1991; Jack D. Jernigan and Steven L. Nock, "Religiosity and Family Stability: Do Families That Pray Together Stay Together?" Department of Sociology, University of Virginia, November 1983.

wisdom, ask our generous God, and He will give it to you."

Verse 3 instructs you to cry out. Plead. Implore. Life is difficult. You've got to admit you could use some understanding on how it all works. We, as believers, have the inside track — *the insight* — that the world desperately wants. Prayer!

Ask, and it will be given to you; seek, and you will find; knock, and it will be opened to you. For everyone who asks receives, and he who seeks finds, and to him who knocks it will be opened.

— Matthew 7:7

Praying together puts God at the center of your marriage. Praying together for wisdom in your life's activities will bring bountiful blessings for a maximum marriage. It's the secret to true wedded bliss!

TAKE ACTION

- Together set an appointed time that you can pray together daily. This is a holy moment, keep it as such.
- Discuss the barriers that might keep you from carrying out this obedience, and encourage one another to be persistent.

PRAY

Him:

- Ask God for wisdom in leading your wife spiritually.
- Ask God for complete understanding in your marriage as well as in His Word.
- Pray specifically for your wife to do well in her job, whatever it may be, and to increase her joy, and her faith.

Her:

- Ask God to bless your husband with diligence in all he does.
- Ask God to give him understanding in his job.
- Ask God for your husband to become even stronger in his faith.

DELIGHTING THE LORD

The Lord *detests the sacrifice of the wicked, but he delights in the prayers of the upright.*

— Proverbs 15:8 (See also Proverbs 15:29; 28:9)

When scripture is repeated several times in the Bible, you can be certain that it's important. This Proverb is worded similarly three different times in Solomon's manual. Take a moment to compare all three of these Proverbs.

What a great expression of God's feelings! For the ones who are not walking with God, He loathes them and is far from them. But for the believer diligently seeking Him, He delights in their prayers and hears them. When I was young, I loved to please my parents and receive their affirmation of a job well done. How much more pleased is our heavenly Father when we walk with Him and talk with Him? He's delighted! He's glad, happy, thrilled, overjoyed, ecstatic!

Being obedient to a daily practice of praying together as a couple will therefore reap extended blessings. Here are four benefits to praying together:

1. Improved obedience. You are commanded to pray persistently and to never give up. Luke 18:1 says, "We should always pray and never give up." Consistent prayers reward you with God's peace.

2. Improved wisdom. Remember James 1:5, "If you need wisdom, ask our generous God, and He will give it to you." And Proverbs 2:6, "For the Lord grants wisdom! From His mouth come knowledge and understanding."

3. Improved communication. Praying with and for your spouse opens a dialog between both of you about your desires and concerns. Ephesians 4:29 confirms this: "...your words will be an encouragement to those who hear them."

4. Improved intimacy.

- *Increased spiritual intimacy.* James 4:8 states, "Come close to God, and God will come close to you."

- *Increased emotional intimacy.* Sharing with each other and with God your heartfelt needs deepens the level of trust and love you have for each other. Hebrews 4:16 explains it this way, "So let us come boldly to the throne of our gracious God. There we will receive His mercy and we will find grace to help us when we need it most."
- *Increased physical intimacy.* When your spiritual and emotional intimacy is enhanced, this will lay the foundation for an increase in desire for one another. Dennis Rainey says, "When spouses pray together, it is about relationship and intimacy, with God *and* with one another."* By praying together, you begin to have a deeper respect and admiration for each other spiritually. Praying together brings romance! You have probably never thought about it that way!

A maximum marriage is one where the husband and wife are a power couple by utilizing the powerful weaponry of prayer which causes the Lord to be delighted. God delights in giving you insights to handle all the issues you face in life.

Therefore confess your sins to each other and pray for each other so that you may be healed. The prayer of a righteous person is powerful and effective.

— James 5:16

TAKE ACTION

- Continue in your efforts to make praying together a daily habit.
- Tell each other how you would like the other to pray for you.

PRAY

Him: • Thank God for delighting in your prayers.

Her: • Thank God for the blessings He gives due to your prayers.

---

* *Two Hearts Praying As One,* Dennis & Barbara Rainey ©2002, Multnomah Books, Colorado Springs, CO

PRAYING HONESTLY

[7]O God, I beg two favors from you; let me have them before I die.
[8]First, help me never to tell a lie. Second, give me neither poverty nor
riches! Give me just enough to satisfy my needs. [9]For if I grow rich, I
may deny you and say, "Who is the LORD?" And if I am too poor, I
may steal and thus insult God's holy name.

— Proverbs 30:7–9

[The 30th chapter of Proverbs is written by Agur, son of Jakeh. It is unknown who he actually is. Some say it is a nickname for Solomon. Some suggest he was a court counselor to Solomon. Others claim it could refer to a tribe. However, the writings are preserved in the Book of Proverbs as God-inspired.]

In the entire book of Proverbs, this lone prayer is recorded. See how simple this prayer is? You don't have to communicate with the God of the universe in eloquent expressions.

This prayer can be a guide for a married couple. Lies are dangerous! Honesty between spouses is mandatory for a maximum marriage. Honesty is about maintaining the integrity of each person in the relationship, which in turn maintains the integrity of the relationship. Being honest with your spouse is vital to opening lines of communication. Even when honesty and truth may make your spouse momentarily uncomfortable, it is essential to communicating and to resolving conflicts which can ultimately mean the difference between developing a strong relationship and growing apart.

It comes down to living a life of integrity. Speak the truth with clarity, love and gentleness. When you dodge the truth out of fear for how it will be received, you only build bigger walls in your relationship. When you tell the truth from a place of love, you're always reinforcing the strength of your connection with your spouse, no matter the response. You have to be honest.

Furthermore, this prayer reflects the qualities of how Jesus teaches us to pray (see Matthew 6:7–13). Especially when it comes to asking God for our daily provisions.

Asking God for more than you really need is being greedy. The greatest danger of wealth is pride, while poverty brings desperation. Having more than you need would tempt you not to need God or rely on Him. Then having too little, or living in poverty, would give you the temptations of envy, stealing, self-pity, fear, discouragement and hopelessness, to name a few.

Paul said he had learned to be content in whatever state he found himself. It didn't matter if we was abounding, and had plenty, or if he was without. He learned to trust God and rely on Him to meet every need in his life. This is similar to the prayer of Agur, as he prayed not to have too little or too much. God wants you to trust Him and not be fearful, as God promises you that He will always take care of your basic needs.

Not that I speak in regard to need, for I have learned in whatever state I am, to be content.
— Philippians 4:11

We serve a big God! Know what you lack in yourself. Ask for something enormous today, and know that God can and will deliver all that you need according to His riches in glory!

TAKE ACTION

- Determine what life situations make you most at risk in distancing yourself from God. Talk about your needs versus your wants.

PRAY

Him: • Ask God for something enormous today.

Her: • Ask God to give you accountability and honesty in all things.
• Thank Him for supplying all your needs.

RECEIVING GOD'S GUIDANCE

Let the wise listen to these proverbs and become even wiser. Let those with understanding receive guidance....
— Proverbs 1:5

From beginning to end, the predominant theme of Proverbs is "wisdom." This does not necessarily mean theoretical knowledge, but it's a genuine discernment between good and evil or right and wrong. To acquire this wisdom is to master lasting success in life. "Understanding" or insight comes from the root meaning "discern" and enables the ability to make right choices.

The first step towards acquiring this knowledge is faith in God (Proverbs 1:7, see page 10). You should have the presence of mind to honor and respect God, to live in awe of His power, and to obey His Word. Proverbs 9:10 further explains that "knowledge of the Holy One results in good judgment."

Wise choices are essential for living a godly life. Bad choices will set you back and you'll suffer the resulting consequences. The wise decision-maker hears God's Word and applies it to his life.

By seeking God, we are able to get clear guidance from Him and thereby reap the benefits of wisdom. Charles Stanley says:

> "Wisdom is the capacity to see things from God's perspective and respond according to scriptural principles....
>
> "Those who walk in wisdom receive the Father's direction for their lives. While God's children still have some painful experiences, they are spared many mistakes and false starts. Biblical principles spare believers numerous wrong decisions and hurtful relationships.
>
> "Nobody is better qualified to guide your steps or lead you to the right path than God.

> "When we walk in divine wisdom, we can rest assured that the Lord is with us always. He won't allow us to enter into any situation that He has not anticipated, nor will He permit a circumstance unless He intends it for our good."*

Here are five Biblical instructions on how to get wisdom:

1. **Fear God** (Proverbs 9:10)
2. **Trust God** (Proverbs 3:5–6)
3. **Pray for Wisdom** (Proverbs 2:3; James 1:5)
4. **Desire Wisdom** (Proverbs 2:4)
5. **Study God's Word** (Joshua 1:8; Psalm 1:2; Psalm 19:7)

The priority status of a maximum marriage is God, front and center. By fearing God, trusting God, praying for God's wisdom, desiring God's wisdom, and studying God's Word, the wise couple is set to receive His guidance in all their ways.

TAKE ACTION

- Read together the verses associated with the five Biblical instructions on how to get wisdom. Make a concentrated effort to apply these in your everyday lives.

PRAY

Him:
- Ask God for daily wisdom for your wife.
- Thank Him for His guidance.

Her:
- Ask God for daily wisdom for your husband.
- Thank Him for His guidance.

**Walking Wisely: Real Guidance for Life's Journey* by Charles F. Stanley, ©2002, Thomas Nelson Publishers, Nashville, TN

RUNNING THE MARATHON

²Tune your ears to wisdom, and concentrate on understanding. ³Cry out for insight, and ask for understanding. ⁴Search for them as you would for silver; seek them like hidden treasures. ⁵Then you will understand what it means to fear the Lord, and you will gain knowledge of God.

— Proverbs 2:2–5

Life is a marathon. It's not a sprint — you can't rush towards getting to the prize without going through a training process. If you approach marriage in the same way, you'll understand it is to be a life-long marathon. It is a continual pursuit of learning about each other, about life, and about growing together spiritually.

You can't expect to run a marathon without training. Marathoners who finish the race have gone through rigorous training day after day in order to prepare themselves for the mission. It takes a continual, conscious effort.

There are some key action words here from Solomon. Notice: tune, concentrate, cry out, ask, search, seek. There is no short-cut in the pursuit of wisdom. In order to pursue God's ideal for your marriage, you must put in the effort to achieve wisdom with actions.

Tune your ears, concentrate. Listen to God's Word. Study thoroughly on how you can apply God's leading in your life.

Cry out, ask. Pray for comprehension on what God wants to tell you.

Search, seek. Just as you would hunt for something extremely valuable, always track down reasoning.

> "Don't expect wisdom to come into your life like great chunks of rock on a conveyor belt. It isn't like that. It's not splashy and bold...nor is it dispensed like a prescription across a counter. Wisdom comes privately from God as a by-product of right decisions, godly reactions, and the application of scriptural principles to daily circumstances. Wisdom comes, for example, not from seeking after a min-

> istry...but more from anticipating the fruit of a disciplined life. Not from trying to do great things for God...but more from being faithful to the small, obscure tasks few people ever see.
>
> "Stop and reflect. Are you just growing old...or are you also growing up? As you 'number your days' do you count just years—the grinding measurement of minutes—or can you find marks of wisdom...character traits that were not there when you were younger?"*

I love the phrase from the above quote: "[Wisdom comes] more from being faithful to the small, obscure tasks few people ever see." If you remain faithful to the process of continually learning, then you'll be in awe of God's amazing gift of knowledge and understanding for you.

Pursuing wisdom has a strong parallel to pursuing a maximum marriage. Be faithful to the small, obscure tasks in your role. Take notice of your spouse's small, obscure tasks and compliment them. Together, you're training for finishing the marathon. Run with purpose in every step. Don't ever give up hunting down hidden treasures of understanding each other. Growing old and wise is what God intends for a long-lasting marriage.

We all have dreams. In order to make dreams come into reality, it takes an awful lot of determination, dedication, self-discipline and effort.

— Jesse Owens, Olympic gold-medalist

TAKE ACTION

- Read 1 Corinthians 9:24–27 and discuss how it relates to today's study from Proverbs.

PRAY

Him: • Ask God for comprehension of His plan for your marriage.

Her: • Ask God for thorough understanding and insight.

---

*Taken from *Growing Strong in the Seasons of Life* by Charles R. Swindoll. Copyright © 1983, 1994, 2007 by Charles R. Swindoll, Inc. Zondervan. www.zondervan.com

SEEKING THE HIDDEN TREASURES

[2]Tune your ears to wisdom, and concentrate on understanding. [3]Cry out for insight, and ask for understanding. [4]Search for them as you would for silver; seek them like hidden treasures. [5]Then you will understand what it means to fear the LORD, and you will gain knowledge of God.

— Proverbs 2:2–5

Let's go on a treasure hunt today and concentrate on verse 4. There are many benefits to having an all out quest for wisdom and understanding. First off, you'll realize this is only for those who fear the Lord — believers in the family of God (v.5). It's our own personal family treasure. Secondly, Solomon likens the hidden treasures to precious metals and gems. Your search for gold is only found in the instruction of God's Word.

Choose my instruction rather than silver, and knowledge rather than pure gold. For wisdom is far more valuable than rubies. Nothing you desire can compare with it.

— Proverbs 8:10–11

How much better to get wisdom than gold, and good judgment than silver!

— Proverbs 16:16

Look at the benefits of seeking the hidden treasures of wisdom (as outlined in verses 7–22 of Proverbs 2):

- Common sense — v. 7a
- A shield of protection — v. 7b
- A guardrail and protection for life's pathways — v. 8
- Discretion and fairness — v. 9
- Joy — v. 10

- Security — v. 11
- Deliverance from crooked people — v. 12–15
- Deliverance from the immoral woman (sin) — v. 16–19
- Enabling of goodness and integrity — v. 20–22

What beautiful treasures to have in your life and marriage! But they won't appear to you automatically. You have to go hunting for them. Effort is required to obtain God's wisdom:

- Hear the Word of God ("tune your ear to wisdom" — Prov. 2:2a)
- Meditate on the Word of God ("concentrate on understanding" — Prov. 2:2b)
- Ask in faith for wisdom ("cry out for insight...ask for understanding" — Prov. 2:3)
- Value its worth ("seek [wisdom and understanding] like hidden treasures" — Prov. 2:4)

With this concentrated effort, you'll not only find wisdom for daily, practical living, but you'll also find Jesus Christ. He will become the center of your marriage relationship. He is the greatest treasure of diligently seeking wisdom!

In Christ lie hidden all the treasures of wisdom and knowledge.
— Colossians 2:3

TAKE ACTION

- Whatever decisions you are facing today or in the near future, make a point to study the Bible for insight for making the right choices.

PRAY

Him: • Thank God for His Son Jesus Christ in giving you the ability to gain knowledge.

Her: • Praise God for the hidden treasures of seeking wisdom.

BUILDING A HOME, Part 1

By wisdom a house is built, and through understanding it is established; through knowledge its rooms are filled with rare and beautiful treasures.

— Proverbs 24:3–4 (NIV)

Here it is — all encompassed in two verses — the secret to building a maximum marriage! Three things are required: **knowledge, understanding,** and **wisdom**. These "building blocks" are the foundation of a fulfilling, godly life. You start with knowledge which gives you information for understanding. But if you don't apply what you've learned, then you don't have wisdom. Wisdom is applying what you've learned. It's not just knowing the information. Remember, wisdom comes from the fear of the Lord (see page 10).

Proverbs stresses the importance of wisdom, knowledge and understanding of God to thrive in our lives (our houses) in order to obtain the blessings of God. It is like the reference Jesus used in Matthew 7:24–27 of the person who builds his house on solid rock (Jesus Christ). When the storms came, the home remained intact. Consequently, the person who doesn't apply God's Word in his life has a weak foundation built on sand. When the storms came, his life collapsed.

Unless the Lord builds the house, those who build it labor in vain.

— Psalm 127:1

Your marriage will only prosper by wisdom and understanding, which is plainly found through the study of scripture. Attending church regularly will only benefit your acquiring of wisdom and counsel from those who are more scholarly than you. If you live by any other means, you are doomed to trouble, pain, and destruction. A God-centered home is strong. Yet without a reverent trust in God, there can't be true wisdom. "For no one can lay any foundation other than…Jesus Christ" (1 Corinthians 3:11).

A wise woman builds her home, but a foolish woman tears it down with her own hands.

— Proverbs 14:1

The wise couple build each other up and make each other stronger in character through godly love. Spouses who tear each other down only destroy their home from within. How do you build up? Choose encouragement over criticism, grace over judgment, and faith over fear.

The blessing of building a marriage on the foundation of God's wisdom, God's understanding, and God's knowledge will bring precious and pleasant riches in the spiritual sense as well as the material sense. God's blessing is on the home that seeks and honors His wisdom.

The blessings that emerge from the wisely-built, godly home is a harmonious loving family, a sense of security, and a sense of stability. So, build your marriage with God's wisdom, establish it with God's understanding, and fill its rooms by the knowledge of God with the pleasant and precious riches of His Word. It will be filled to overflowing, you can be sure.

Do your planning and prepare your fields before building your house.

— Proverbs 24:27

TAKE ACTION

- Read Matthew 7:24–27 for further study.

PRAY

Him: • Ask God for knowledge, understanding and wisdom in all your husbandly decisions.

Her: • Ask God for knowledge, understanding and wisdom in all your wifely decisions.

BUILDING A HOME, Part 2

Wisdom has built her house; she has carved its seven columns.
— Proverbs 9:1

This Proverb further shows that a house of wisdom is built on the mighty foundational strength of God and supported by seven columns. Yesterday's study was on the three foundational building blocks: **knowledge, understanding,** and **wisdom.** Today, we'll build on those blocks with seven columns. But what are the seven columns? There are many speculations as to what they might be.

In the previous chapter, Solomon describes seven attributes of wisdom in 8:12–14 (NKJV): "I, wisdom, dwell with **prudence,** and I find **knowledge and discretion.** [13]**The fear of the LORD** is hatred of evil. Pride and arrogance and the way of evil and perverted speech I hate. [14]I have **counsel** and **sound wisdom;** I have **insight;** I have **strength.**" These could be the seven columns he mentions in 9:1.

In the New Testament, perhaps James describes these seven pillars as well, using somewhat different words: "But the wisdom that is from above is first **pure,** then **peaceable, gentle, willing to yield, full of mercy and good fruits, without partiality** and **without hypocrisy**" (James 3:17 NKJV). I'm going to use James' list and show how the inspired Word of God spans the one thousand years between Solomon's and James' writings. These characteristics should always be present in a maximum marriage home. The first four columns will be studied today. The remaining three will be tomorrow in "Building a Home, Part 3."

1. Purity — The first column James lists is the central column, the one that carries more weight than any of the others. It is the home where our Holy God is in the center. This household's priority is fearing God. And we should strive for that purity in ourselves. Psalm 119:9–11 wisely tells us: "How can a young person stay pure? By obeying your word. I have tried hard to find you — don't let me wander from your commands. I have hidden your word in my heart, that I might not sin against you."

In Proverbs 8:13, Solomon confirms the fear of the Lord, or reverence, as one of the seven elements of wisdom.

The remaining six columns are the surrounding outside pillars of the home.

2. Peaceableness — Peaceableness is a state of being calm, tranquil, or peaceful. Isaiah 32:18 describes this environment, "My people will live in safety, quietly at home. They will be at rest." What a beautiful description of a godly home!

Solomon also describes one of the pillars as sound wisdom. This can be related to your everyday behavior. Are you a peaceful person?

3. Gentleness — See a further study of "Expressing Gentleness" on pages 62–65. Understand that this fruit is not a weak quality but one of strength, as Solomon validates in the last part of 8:14.

4. Reasonableness — This means the fact of being based on or using good judgment and therefore being fair and practical. Philippians 4:5 says, "Let your reasonableness be known to everyone." It's a quality of good sense. It means you are open to reason, that you are teachable.

Proverbs 8:12 confirms this attribute in "prudence." When you have prudence, you have self-restraint and sound judgment, or reasonableness. The godly man is a man who takes an interest in all those things going on about him; he plans his course of actions realistically. Proverbs 22:3: "A prudent person foresees danger and takes precautions."

THE HOME THAT WISDOM BUILT

TAKE ACTION

- Dedicate your home to constantly striving for the seven pillars of wisdom, starting with making sure that everything you do in the home is God-centered (Purity).

BUILDING A HOME, Part 3

Wisdom has built her house; she has carved its seven columns.
— Proverbs 9:1

Continuing our study of the seven columns from yesterday, we'll see how the house of wisdom in a maximum marriage can be such a solid superstructure.

5. Full of mercy and good fruits — James' fifth attribute of wisdom from above is one that Christ resembled. A person who is full of mercy has no problem forgiving anyone, freely and cheerfully from the heart. They exercise compassion towards others and express the fruit of the Spirit (Galatians 5:22–23). They make an effort to do good to others at all times.

Solomon could have thought the same in saying wisdom is full of counsel. A merciful person is one who can give good advice, and model the advice they give. They also seek counsel in their own life.

6. Without partiality — An impartial person is one who is described as fair and kind. He will be wholehearted and straightforward. He will not be double-minded, but strong in faith in God, and he won't be looking at his own weaknesses, but at the promises of God. He is a dependable person.

Solomon backs it up with the description of knowledge and discretion. This wise person is someone who possesses or shows sound judgment and keen perception.

7. Without hypocrisy — Constructing the last column of wisdom in your life means having sincerity or the quality of being free from deceit. This person is honest, genuine, truthful, and demonstrates integrity. They have a strong desire to live according to God's truths.

This characteristic produces understanding. An understanding person is one with insight. Solomon reiterates this in Proverbs 4:7, "The beginning of wisdom is this: Get wisdom, and whatever you get, get insight" (ESV).

If you need wisdom, ask our generous God, and he will give it to you. He will not rebuke you for asking.
— James 1:5

In Scripture, the number seven is often used to represent spiritual perfection. Building the seven columns into a maximum marriage means your home will always be under construction. You must be diligent in seeking God's spiritual wisdom every day. It is by continually pursing wisdom you are building onward and upward. Being obedient to the pursuit will result in having a strong and blessed home.

TAKE ACTION

- Concentrate on practicing one column characteristic per day this week. In one week you'll acquire wisdom in a stronger relationship and home life.

PRAY

Him: • Thank God for the ability to build these qualities.

Her: • Thank God for His generosity in giving you wisdom.

WISDOM'S SEVEN COLUMNS

James 3:17	Proverbs 8:12–14
• Purity	• Fear of the LORD
• Peaceableness	• Sound wisdom
• Gentleness	• Strength
• Reasonableness	• Prudence
• Full of mercy and good fruits	• Counsel
• Impartiality	• Knowledge and discretion
• Sincerity	• Insight

There could be other interpretations of the seven columns since Proverbs and the Bible are full of definitions of wisdom. These two sets of attributes from James 3 and Proverbs 8 work together and overlap each other in many ways.

LOVING YOURSELF

To acquire wisdom is to love yourself; people who cherish understanding will prosper.

— Proverbs 19:8

Jesus said you should love your neighbor as yourself (Matt. 22:39). Paul wrote that each husband "must love his wife as he loves himself" (Eph. 5:33). Solomon says to acquire wisdom is to love yourself. Loving yourself means you have a good self-image. Loving yourself means you want the best for yourself. You care about your well-being.

This is not about a selfish, self-centered love — your accomplishments, your popularity, your power, or your wealth. That kind of self-love is dangerous and does not represent the love of God.

You are extremely important to God. He loves you, values you, and desires a close relationship with you. He has a specific plan for your life. This should give you confidence and a strong self-image.

At the very core of your self-image is the desire to be loved and be regarded as lovable. When you accept that God loves you unconditionally, you have the basis for healthy, godly self-esteem.

A proper, healthy love for yourself will lead to generosity and selfless giving. Knowing and having the confidence of God's unconditional love will allow you to love others unconditionally. You'll place no requirements on them in order to receive your love. God loves and approves of you, just as you are. Therefore, you should approve of you. Look at the following truths that identify your value to God.

- You are His masterpiece (Eph. 2:10 NLT, also Psalm 139:13–14).
- You are completely forgiven (Col. 1:14, also Psalm 103:12).
- You can be confident that the good work that God has begun in you will be perfected (Phil. 1:6).
- You are loved by God with an everlasting love (Jer. 31:3).
- God will calm all your fears and rejoices over you (Zeph. 3:17).
- You are adopted as God's child (Eph. 1:5, also John 1:12).
- You have been made right in God's sight by faith (Rom. 5:1 NLT).
- You are holy, blameless, beyond reproach (Col. 1:22 NASB, also Heb. 3:1).

- You can do everything through Christ who gives you strength (Phil. 4:13).
- You have been rescued from Satan's domain and transferred into the kingdom of Christ (Col. 1:13).
- You have been made complete in Christ (Col. 2:10).
- You have been given a spirit of power, love, and self-discipline (2 Tim. 1:7).
- You are assured that all things are working together for good (Rom. 8:28).
- You are free from condemning charges against you (Rom. 8:31).
- You cannot be separated from the love of God (Rom. 8:35).

If these don't boost your self-esteem, I don't know what will.

Acquiring wisdom will add benefits to your self-perception. According to Proverbs 8:32-35, you will be blessed, find life, and obtain favor from the Lord. Who wouldn't want God's blessings and joy for their life? Always be in a learning mode about God's Word.

In the second part of today's Proverb, he uses the word cherish. In order to cherish something — in this case, understanding — you hold it in high esteem. To cherish is a notch above love. You truly treasure it. The benefit? A prosperous life. A prosperous marriage.

Acquire wisdom. Cherish understanding. A maximum marriage is continually seeking these attributes because the husband and wife love themselves. They realize they are perfected in the image of Christ and thereby have the confidence to extend His love to each other.

TAKE ACTION

- Put your spouse's name in the identity traits listed above and read them out loud to him or her. You'll boost each other's esteem and come to see the other as God sees them.

PRAY

Him:
- Thank God you are His masterpiece.
- Ask Him for wisdom and understanding.

Her:
- Thank God that He calms all your fears and rejoices over you.
- Ask Him for complete confidence in your abilities as He has made you.

READING THE BOOK

Every word of God proves true. He is a shield to all who come to him for protection.

— Proverbs 30:5

Have you ever thought of just how great the Bible is? This document has been handed down through the ages and is still relevant for today. What a privilege we have to read it daily! In it are all the answers to life's emotional battles. Anything you face in life can be eased through God's promises in His Word. Simple sentences can encourage and strengthen. Complete stories of individuals help us live for God and show how He wants what is best for us. And He will bless us if we obey his truths spelled out in the Word. It's all about relationships, with each other, and with Him. It is an entire study of psychology at its best.

When I was very young, my grandparents kept a huge Bible on the side table next to their couch. They read it everyday. One day I set something on top of that Bible. And my grandmother lovingly and gently took that item off and said, "This is God's Word. It is valuable. Nothing is to ever be set on top of it." Right there, I learned the true value of the Book. And to this day, I never set anything on top of it.

How sad for anyone not to believe in the Bible! Life is difficult enough, why make it harder? In some countries, the Bible is banned and you can be arrested if you have one. A late missionary friend of mine, Jeff Lauer, had the joy of passing out Bibles to students in foreign countries who never had one. They craved it. We can easily purchase one at Walmart or have it for free on our phone.*

All scripture is God-breathed.

— 2 Timothy 3:16a (NIV)

Consider the fact that the Bible is comprised of 66 books written over a period of about 1,500 years by over 40 authors from all

---

*From *Minutes in His Presence, 52 Devotionals for Men* by Dennis R. Davidson, Copyright © 2018

walks of life, with different kinds of personalities, and in all sorts of situations. It was written in three languages on three continents, and it covers hundreds of controversial subjects. Yet, it fits together into one cohesive story with an appropriate beginning, a logical ending, a central character, and a consistent theme. Find *any* other 66 books off the library shelf in the religious section and see if every one of them are in harmony with each other. You can't. It hasn't been done. The Bible is totally unique. "It is useful to teach us what is true and to make us realize what is wrong in our lives. It corrects us when we are wrong and teaches us to do what is right. God uses it to prepare His people to do every good work" (2 Timothy 3:16b NLT).

Today's Proverb tells of the true value of God's Word. It becomes our shield of protection in the battles we face each day. What could be better than going into battle with a God-shield? If a marriage is struggling, the husband and wife who are daily probing the Bible will find their strength by trusting God's truths. A maximum marriage is one that reads and studies The Book, not just during crises, but every day.

Study this Book of Instruction continually. Meditate on it day and night so you will be sure to obey everything written in it. Only then will you prosper and succeed in all you do.

— Joshua 1:8

TAKE ACTION

- Make a practice of diving into the Bible every day. While reading a chapter or two a day is good, make a point to study particular verses by cross referencing and with a Study Bible. Your reading of this devotional book is a great practice, but only meant to be a supplemental study to your daily reading. Daily practice will reveal God's voice and direction. Guaranteed!

PRAY

Him: • Thank God that you can hear His voice through His Word.

Her: • Ask God to give you the desire to delight in His Word.

ENCOURAGING WORDS ENERGIZE

The words of the godly are a life-giving fountain; the words of the wicked conceal violent intentions.

— Proverbs 10:11

There is tremendous power in your words. Picture in your mind a life-giving fountain. I think one would want to drink from it frequently. You have the power to offer that revitalizing water in everything you say to another — especially your spouse. No one likes to be around someone who constantly puts them down. On the other hand, you'll gravitate to someone who builds you up and encourages you.

Well-chosen words that affirm and build up are eloquent. We love to receive them. Solomon says in Proverbs 10:20 "the words of the godly are like sterling silver." Then in the next verse he says, "words of the godly encourage many." And if you still haven't gotten his point, in verse 32 of the same chapter he says that the "godly speak helpful words."

How can you offer this life-giving fountain to your spouse? Be watchful of the positive things they do. If you focus on negatives, then more than likely, negative hurtful words will come out of your mouth. Don't try to outdo one another with put-downs or sarcasm. It's unfortunate that those who are closest to us are often the last to get encouragement from us.

Be deliberate in expressing positive affirmation. If your husband is worried about a presentation he must make at his company, cheer him up by stating you believe in him. Shaunti Feldhahn says, "If a woman believes in her husband, he can conquer the world — or at least his little corner of it."* If your wife is exhausted by all the busyness in her life, let her know you are supportive and appreciate her diligence and perseverance.

**For Women Only* by Shaunti Feldhahn ©2004, 2013 by Veritas Enterprises, Inc. Published by Multnomah Books.

...an encouraging word cheers a person up.

— Proverbs 12:25b

Nobody's words are more important than parents' words to their children. A maximum marriage is filled with encouraging words between the parents and also from the parents to the kids. A timely "Good job!" energizes and affirms a child to keep at it. Do you want to motivate your children to excel in schoolwork or in their chores around the house? Tell them the good job they are doing. If they've failed in some area, you can still build them up with a kind word of understanding. Life-giving words build character.

We have the choice to choose words that are godly or wicked. Hurtful words tear down and destroy. Encouraging words offer strength and life.

The tongue can bring death or life...

— Proverbs 18:21

Let no corrupting talk come out of your mouths, but only such as is good for building up, as fits the occasion, that it may give grace to those who hear.

— Ephesians 4:29

TAKE ACTION

- Make an effort to start practicing praising each other.
- Start saying "please" and "thank you" more often.

PRAY

Him:
- Ask God to help you use words that are pleasing and uplifting.
- Name some positive attributes in your wife and thank God for them.

Her:
- Ask God to help you see the good in your husband and to praise him for what he does.

KIND WORDS SATISFY, Part 1

Kind words are like honey — sweet to the soul and healthy for the body.

— Proverbs 16:24

In recent years, medical research has discovered there is actual medicinal truth behind this Proverb. Genuine kindness creates feelings of warmth and connection, as does love, and these feelings produce the hormone called oxytocin in our bodies.

Oxytocin is a cardio-protective hormone. It provides protection to the cardiovascular system. First, it stimulates production of nitric oxide, which then dilates our arteries. The result is a reduction in blood pressure. Second, oxytocin acts as both an antioxidant and anti-inflammatory throughout the cardiovascular system. We're encouraged to have antioxidants in our diets through eating vegetables, fruits, and things like cinnamon, dark chocolate, and even olive oil.

Since oxytocin is a potent cardio-protective hormone and since we naturally produce it when we're being genuinely kind, we can therefore say that kindness is protective of the heart. Kindness reduces blood pressure, acts as an antioxidant, and is an anti-inflammatory.

You have probably felt that relaxing, calming sense that kindness brings, whether you're the person being kind, the recipient of it, or even a witness to it. Even sometimes you'll notice a warm feeling in the chest, which is caused by an oxytocin-stimulated increase in blood flow to the heart. There is validity behind writing "I love you" with a ♥!

Oxytocin also helps speed up the healing of wounds. When oxytocin levels are low, certain wounds can take longer to heal.

This natural hormone of kindness also has been shown to act as an antioxidant in our skin cells. Getting plenty of oxytocin slows the aging of skin. We can only produce this hormone through how we feel, which is often a consequence of how we behave. Therefore, there's a strong case for the effect of being kind and how we age. This makes sense because we know that stress can speed up aging.

Research has also shown that bringing up a child in a warm emotional environment has positive effects on growth and development.

A maximum marriage exhibits kindness in various deeds, as well as in speech. Love and kindness *can* mend a broken heart, but more than just emotional healing, these feelings have very positive physical effects too, on the heart and the entire body.

Kindness really does heal! God has created us in His very own image of kindness.

The words I love to hear from my wife when I do some act of kindness are, "You're awesome!" These kind words are sweet to my soul *and* healthy for my body, as well as hers.

Let your speech always be gracious, seasoned with salt, so that you may know how you ought to answer each person.

— Colossians 4:6 (ESV)

The right words bring satisfaction.

— Proverbs 18:20b

▩ TAKE ACTION

- As Romans 12:10 (ESV) tells us to "outdo one another in showing honor," make a point to do acts of kindness for each other. Then express kind words acknowledging the other's kind acts.
- Place a sticky note with "I ♥ you!" in a conspicuous place that will make their day.

▩ PRAY

Him:
- Thank God for the many acts of kindness your wife provides.
- Ask God to give you the mentality to express kind words on a regular basis.

Her:
- Thank God for the healing effects of kindness.
- Thank God for your husband's providing of kindness.

KIND WORDS SATISFY, Part 2

A word fitly spoken is like apples of gold in a setting of silver.
— Proverbs 25:11 (ESV)

There are sayings in our everyday world that downplay the significance of words: Talk is cheap; Actions speak louder than words; A picture is worth a thousand words; Sticks and stones may break my bones but words will never hurt me. What a waste we make of words. They gush out of us like a torrent, void of redeeming qualities. We speak before we think. We wound people carelessly. But Solomon declares there is high value in rightly used words. The right word from the right person at the right time is exquisite.

Everyone enjoys a fitting reply; it is wonderful to say the right thing at the right time!
— Proverbs 15:23

We live in a world where people can be very cruel and use hateful, disrespectful and painful words to put others down. There is a false assumption that it makes one feel better by doing so. This paints an ugly picture. In contrast, relevant words paint a beautiful picture. Just think of ripe, golden apples glowing on a silver platter. How appetizing and luscious! Relevant words are words of encouragement. Words that are kind and comforting. They're pure gold.

Encourage each other and build each other up.
— 1 Thessalonians 5:11

Kindness is contagious. Spoken compliments will, in theory, inspire the recipient to give out a compliment to another. Then that person will be inspired to do the same, and so on. It can be a ripple effect. It's amazing to think about how positive affirmations can snowball. A beautiful domino effect can result. It's pure gold!

The difference between the right word and the almost right word is the difference between lightning and a lightning bug.

— Mark Twain

Words satisfy the mind as much as fruit does the stomach; good talk is as gratifying as a good harvest. [21] *Words kill, words give life; they're either poison or fruit—you choose.*

— Proverbs 18:20-21 (THE MESSAGE) (See also Proverbs 12:14a)

Kind words are like a luscious fruit. Mouth-watering. Succulent. Your words are important. Make them count. J. B. Phillips correctly assessed the impact of words when he wrote: "If words are to enter men's hearts and bear fruit, they must be the right words shaped cunningly to pass men's defenses and explode silently and effectually within their minds."

The finest example of that are the words and phrases of Jesus Christ. Being the ultimate word-smith, Jesus used some of His most significant words in a brief statement we call the Golden Rule: "Therefore, however you want people to treat you, so treat them, for this is the Law and the Prophets" (Matt. 7:12).

Choose words that save, and love, and heal. Decrease volume and increase value. A word is a terrible thing to waste.

TAKE ACTION

- Today, build your spouse up with an encouraging word or compliment. And then again tomorrow. And then the next day, and so on.

PRAY

Him: • Pray Psalm 19:14, "May the words of my mouth and the meditation of my heart be pleasing to you, O Lord, my rock and my redeemer."

Her: • Ask God to give you loving words to use daily.

COMPLIMENTING AND PRAISING

Worry weighs a person down; an encouraging word cheers a person up.
— Proverbs 12:25

Have you ever had a parent, teacher, or a coach cheer you on when you think you couldn't accomplish a task? The mere encouragement — the outright belief they had in you — spurred you on to a greater performance.

Encouraging compliments are a powerful force. When received, they lift you up when you're down. They boost your morale. They make you happier. They are kindness in action.

My own mother was an encourager. She was continually building others up and complimenting them. I once challenged her to say something good about the devil. She thought for a moment, then said, "He's a hard worker." Find the good in others — it's there if you look.

Not only should you compliment your spouse's accomplishments and achievements, but compliment their physical attractiveness as well. The husband and wife who continually encourage each other and build each other up with compliments will have a stronger, long-lasting love. Show appreciation of your spouse. Compliment their attributes.

Her husband praises her: "There are many virtuous and capable women in the world, but you surpass them all!"
— Proverbs 31: 28b–29

You are beautiful, my darling, beautiful beyond words.
— Song of Songs 4:1

My lover is dark and dazzling, better than ten thousand others!
— Song of Songs 5:16

Here are four reasons you should shower compliments on others, especially your spouse:

- Compliments motivate — Whoever you praise with positive, uplifting comments will be motivated to excel even more.
- Compliments create positivity — Focusing on and verbally expressing about someone's good qualities does you, as well as them, good. It makes for an optimistic outlook on life.
- Compliments spread love — Expressing appreciation for someone's deeds are bonding. It makes a connection stronger and makes you more lovable in their eyes.
- Compliments boost self-esteem — It does not require any physical effort to praise someone's skill or appearance but this little thing can build up their self-esteem and you'll start feeling great about yourself, too.

"Words of affirmation" is one of the five love languages. Whether or not it is your spouse's particular love language, flood them with sincere words that encourage and build up. Because it'll cheer them up. And it'll cheer you up as well.

TAKE ACTION

- Read Song of Songs 4:1–5 and 5:10–16. Take note of how the husband compliments his wife's physical attributes and how the wife does the same. See also Song of Songs 7:1–9 for their expressions of sexual compliments.
- On the following pages is a list of compliments you can give to someone. Go out and give someone a gentle compliment today. And start with your spouse. Make them smile. Make their day.

PRAY

Him:
- Praise God for your wife's achievements.
- Name specific accomplishments that make you proud of your wife.

Her:
- Praise God for your husband's positive qualities.
- Thank God for your husband's encouraging words.

A list of compliments that will make someone smile.

Complimenting Positivity
These compliments focus on the joy, fun, and positive outlook the person brings.

1. Your smile is contagious.
2. Your positive viewpoint is great.
3. You have the best laugh.
4. You light up the room.
5. You have a great sense of humor.
6. I look up to you because you have charm.
7. You're like sunshine on a rainy day.
8. You bring out the best in other people.
9. I love your cheerful outlook.
10. My world is brighter when you're around.
11. You're so much fun to be around.
12. Jokes are funnier when you tell them.
13. You always know how to find that silver lining.
14. You're a candle in the darkness.
15. Being around you is like a happy little vacation.
16. You're countenance is comforting to be around.
17. You're like a breath of fresh air.
18. You're always making someone smile.
19. You have a warm personality.

Complimenting Personal Traits
These compliments acknowledge different qualities the person exhibits.

20. You have impeccable manners.
21. I like your style.
22. You're strong.
23. Your mojo is incredible.
24. Your kindness is so uplifting.
25. You are brave.
26. Your inner character is beautiful.
27. You have the courage of your convictions.
28. You're a great listener.
29. You are very distinguished.
30. Your cleverness is attractive.
31. You're inspiring.
32. You're so thoughtful.
33. You set out to accomplish your goals.
34. You exude confidence.

Complimenting Intelligence, Creativity, and Resourcefulness
These compliments show that you appreciate the person's abilities.

35. You're a smart cookie.
36. Your perspective is refreshing.
37. Your common sense is impressive.
38. Your perception of things is always positive.
39. You have the best ideas.
40. You're always learning new things to better yourself.
41. You have impeccable creativity.
42. You are worthy of respect.
43. When you make a mistake, you fix it.
44. You're great at figuring stuff out.
45. Your creative potential seems limitless.
46. Your energy level is amazing.
47. You have a good head on your shoulders.
48. Nothing keeps you down.

Complimenting Accomplishments
It is often good to compliment a specific action or achievement.

49. You should be proud of yourself.
50. You are making a difference.

51. You deserve a hug right now.
52. You're a great example to others.
53. Actions speak louder than words, and yours tell an incredible story.

Complimenting Personal Relationships

These compliments focus on how the person relates to others.

54. You're an awesome friend.
55. You're more helpful than you realize.
56. Hanging out with you is always fun.
57. It's amazing how you always say the right things.
58. Being around you makes everything better.
59. You should be thanked more often. Thank you.
60. Our community is better because you're in it.
61. You're always supporting someone's ideas.
62. You always know just what to say.
63. The people you love are lucky to have you in their lives.
64. Any team would be lucky to have you on it.
65. People are drawn to you because of your kindness.
66. The way you treasure your loved ones is incredible.
67. You're a gift to those around you.

Complimenting Appearance

These compliments are meant for someone close to you. They should be avoided in business and social contexts.

68. You're gorgeous.
69. You look great today.
70. Your eyes are so breathtaking.
71. You always look great.
72. That color is perfect on you.
73. You smell really good.
74. You're mesmerizing.
75. You have a cute nose.
76. You are God's masterpiece.
77. Your hair looks stunning.
78. Your voice is magnificent.
79. You're awesome in every way.
80. Your hair is radiant.
81. Your lips are so kissable.

Complimenting the Whole Person

These compliments may be more general. As with complimenting appearance, consider whether they are appropriate or may be bordering on being flirtatious.

82. I appreciate you.
83. You are pretty much perfect.
84. You are enough.
85. You're so elegant.
86. You are praiseworthy at all times.
87. You've got all the right moves.
88. Everything would be better if more people were like you.
89. I love your compassion.
90. You're wonderful.
91. You're such a thoughtful person.
92. You're one of a kind.
93. Your friendliness is the best.
94. You display grace.
95. You're always dependable.
96. You can always be counted on to live up to your word.
97. Your laugh is comforting.
98. You're very personable.
99. You're down to earth and real.
100. You're really something special.

Adapted from 100 Positivity-Boosting Compliments by Nataly Kogan. Updated May 14, 2019. verywellmind.com

EXPRESSING GENTLENESS, Part 1

Gentle words are a tree of life; a deceitful tongue crushes the spirit.
— Proverbs 15:4

In Proverbs, the "tree of life" is mentioned four times (3:18; 11:30; 13:12; 15:4). This imagery is used as a metaphor for wisdom and for good qualities you can possess. It's an accessible and abundant source of blessing. A tree that is alive is beautiful. A dead tree is not.

When you live by God's Word every day with love and godliness, people around you are blessed, and there is growth of character. A maximum marriage reflects this blessing through wisdom, and as indicated here, gentle words.

In order to speak gentle words, you have to be gentle in the first place. Gentleness means being even-tempered; considerate; honorable, and strength under control. As one of the nine "fruit of the spirit" (Galatians 5:22-23), gentleness is sometimes viewed as a weak value. Being gentle is often associated with giving in or simply being nice. True gentleness couldn't be further from the truth.

Gentleness can be found in many forms. It's quiet, but strong. Here are 10 ways it can be practiced in a maximum marriage.

1. Gentleness is choosing to address difficult issues during the day instead of at night.
2. Gentleness is honoring the free will of your spouse, but does not join in just to pacify them.
3. Gentleness is speaking the truth in love. It shines a light on a tender issue while maintaining respect.
4. Gentleness is remaining even-tempered during a crisis, yet staying alert for possible dangers.
5. Gentleness is offering a hug when your spouse messes up, and saying nothing.
6. Gentleness uses light humor to diffuse tense moments.
7. Gentleness protects vulnerable spots but addresses the hurt that needs healing.

8. Gentleness never needs to yell, and never cowers or whimpers.
9. Gentleness takes its time to consider all the facts, but is quick to ask for forgiveness.
10. Gentleness remains ever present, even if it's never acknowledged.*

Anger can be the opposite of gentleness. Think about "chilling" or "calming down" before spouting off if you're upset. Words spoken in anger will be the best speech you'll ever regret. A raised voice will do more to push your spouse away and to crush their spirit rather than bringing them closer to your side.

Gentle words are quiet, calm, peaceful words. They are more convincing, more compelling, and more prevailing. A tree of life blessing.

A gentle answer deflects anger, but harsh words make tempers flare.
— Proverbs 15:1

The heart of the godly thinks carefully before speaking; the mouth of the wicked overflows with evil words.
— Proverbs 15:28

TAKE ACTION

- In Matthew 11:29 Jesus describes himself as being humble and gentle at heart. Practice the art of gentleness by saying things to each other that are quiet and peaceful.

PRAY

Him:
- Ask God to calm your aggressive temper if you have one.
- Thank God for the sweet nature of your wife.

Her:
- Ask God to help you to use words of love and gentleness, never nagging.
- Thank God for giving you an honorable husband.

*© EncourageYourSpouse.com. "10 Ways to Show Gentleness in Marriage." Nov. 15, 2012

EXPRESSING GENTLENESS, Part 2

Some people make cutting remarks, but the words of the wise bring healing.

— Proverbs 12:18

There seems to be an unfortunate trend within social media to criticize others. Comments may be put out there just to ignite critical responses. People seem to love to put others down, as if they are the perfect ones. What does the Bible say about criticism?

- Don't judge others. (Matthew 7:1-2)
- Don't jump to conclusions. (Proverbs 25:8)
- Don't speak evil against each others. (1 Peter 3:10b; James 4:11-12)
- Do everything in love. (1 Corinthians 16:14)
- Speak words of life, not death. (Proverbs 12:18)
- Your goal should be to help, not hurt. (Hebrews 10:24)
- Leave it to God. (Romans 14:4)
- Always remember: God's in control. (Proverbs 3:5-6)

Fittingly, it's rather difficult to criticize with gentle words. If you try it, you might notice that the other person will take your words harshly, no matter your intent to be gentle. Especially in social media. You cannot hear tone in a post or in a text. But can you really say, "You are an idiot" in a gentle, loving way?

Encouraging words build up self-esteem and confidence in another. Negative comments will demoralize and de-spirit a person. Notice how "You are awesome" has a totally different outcome than the derogatory statement in the previous paragraph. "You are awesome!" You can whisper it. You can yell it. It still comes across as gentleness.

Everyone enjoys a fitting reply; it is wonderful to say the right thing at the right time!

— Proverbs 15:23

Gentle words, quiet words, are after all the most powerful words. They are more convincing, more compelling, more prevailing.

— Washington Gladden, American Congregational pastor

Let's not fall into the same trap that the world does of being critical of others. Jesus condemned an attitude of self-righteousness that makes you care nothing about the souls of others. Let's pray for others, build them up, and compliment instead of criticize.

TAKE ACTION

- Look up each of the scriptures in today's first paragraph and write them individually on sticky-notes. Put the notes around where you will see them throughout the day — on your mirror, on your car dashboard, on the refrigerator, on your desk, on your monitor.
- Do the same with some of the compliments on pages 60–61 for your spouse to find in a surprise.

PRAY

Him:

- Ask God to give you a mindset of spreading gentleness around with your words.
- If you've ever thought of yourself as better than others, ask God for forgiveness.

Her:

- Ask God to help you be uplifting and encouraging to those around you, especially your husband.
- Thank God for giving you friends who are gentle with you.

OFFERING SOLUTIONS

The wise are glad to be instructed, but babbling fools fall flat on their faces.

— Proverbs 10:8

We often tend to dwell on problems in our marriage rather than solve them. Have you ever complained about something your spouse is doing that's not right or something they should be doing?

Psychologists Les and Leslie Parrot say, "The real way to make progress when faced with a problem is not to dwell on it by pointing an accusing finger, but to solve it by proposing a commanding solution.... This proverb implies that the wise person is more likely to hear a thoughtful, commanding solution than to listen to a "chattering fool" who simply talks on and on, criticizing and nagging."*

The "instructor" is key in how the "instructee" responds. The words *command* and *commend* are very similar in nature. A successful commander is one who also commends. When a directive is desired to be carried out, it is more likely to be followed when a person is commended for their achievements and good efforts.

The mouth of the godly person gives wise advice...

— Proverbs 10:31a

Perhaps there is no greater motivator than a sincere compliment. Words of affirmation can go a long way in the positive growth of someone. The giver of advice must understand how to give counsel through words that build up and praise. Sentences with too many words put a fog over the instruction.

A truly wise person uses few words...

— Proverbs 17:27a

---

* *Proverbs for Couples*, Les & Leslie Parrot, ©1997, Zondervan Publishing

Additionally, there is the listener of instruction. Husbands and wives must be good listeners with discernment. A levelheaded person loves advice and is happy to receive it. This conscientious maturity allows them to grow stronger in character. As James 1:19 tells us, "Be quick to listen and slow to speak." A good listener discerns and processes the advice given. They never retaliate with an insult or put-down.

Get all the advice and instruction you can.
— Proverbs 19:20

Fools think their own way is right, but the wise listen to others.
— Proverbs 12:15

A maximum marriage is one where both the husband and wife share insights in a positive manner that will improve circumstances, not create crises. Don't command, but commend.

▒ TAKE ACTION

- Be bold enough to ask each other where you need to improve in some area of life and offer solutions.
- Take turns commending each other on a attribute.

▒ PRAY

Him:
- Ask God help you grow in an area where you may be weak.
- Thank God for the wisdom and common sense of your wife.

Her:
- Ask God to guide you in improving yourself and to learn how to use words that commend.

MANAGING YOUR MOUTH

Put away from you crooked speech, and put devious talk far from you.
— Proverbs 4:24 (ESV)

What a waste you can make of your words. They can cascade out like a waterfall, void of redeeming qualities. You can wound people carelessly with what you say to them. Words can hurt!

Proverbs 18:21 says it best, "Death and Life are in the power of the tongue." That places an extremely important premium on the words we speak.

Notice the words used in today's verse. "Crooked" and "devious" are not words that show grace. What does a crooked word look like? The Hebrew meaning of "crooked" means the act of perverting something by turning it to a wrong use. Speech is supposed to bless people and show them to Jesus. Our words are supposed to lift people into the realm of God. Speech, which is supposed to bless but instead curses, is crooked speech.

Psalm 10:3, 7 (ESV) explains it this way "For the wicked boasts of the desires of his soul, and the one greedy for gain curses and renounces the LORD.... His mouth is filled with cursing and deceit and oppression; under his tongue are mischief and iniquity." Look at the list the Psalmist gives for crooked speech. The mouth of the wicked is filled with crooked speech. It includes...

- Cursing
- Deceit
- Oppression
- Mischief
- Iniquity

Cursing is filthy language. Deceit is lying. Oppression is cruel and abusive speech. Mischief is being disobedient and iniquity means wickedness. These are not godly traits. These are the traits of a "worthless, wicked man" (See Proverbs 6:12–19). As far as God is concerned, anything coming out your mouths that disagree with His Word is devious (warped and twisted), unruly, obnoxious and deceitful. These words only leave damage in their wake.

Fill your mind with godly thoughts and your words will follow appropriately. Godly words will have the attributes of:

- Love
- Peace
- Kindness
- Mercy
- Honesty
- Goodness

Be aware of how you talk to your spouse. If it's not godly, it's sinful and abusive. Think before you speak, and if you've allowed your conversation to become negative and unscriptural by habit, make the decision today to change that!

A man of knowledge uses words with restraint.
— Proverbs 17:27

To speak ill of others is a dishonest way of praising ourselves.
— Will Durant

TAKE ACTION

- Take note of all the negative things you say in a day.
- Make a point to turn that around and keep track of times you say positive and kind things to each other.

PRAY

Him:
- Ask God to fill your mind with godly thoughts and words.
- Thank God for a particular characteristic you like about your wife.

Her:
- Thank God for a personality trait your husband has.

LISTENING EFFECTIVELY

Spouting off before listening to the facts is both shameful and foolish.
— Proverbs 18:13

The art of listening is an effective skill for good communication and resolving conflicts. When your spouse talks to you, do you really listen? Do you concentrate on what they're saying? Or do you contemplate what you are going to say back before they finish?

You express your love to your spouse best when you really listen. Real listening involves making eye contact. By looking into your spouse's eyes when they speak will allow you to see volumes that you would never hear just from your ears. Show them that you are actively listening to the conversation.

Understand this, my dear brothers and sisters: You must all be quick to listen, slow to speak, and slow to get angry.
— James 1:19

One of the most effective listening exercises is the active listening method coined by Thomas Gordon, author of Parent Effectiveness Training. In this method, the speaker expresses his or her thoughts or feelings. Then the listener repeats back to the speaker the thoughts or the feelings expressed. Next the listener asks the speaker if he or she has accurately understood and restated what the speaker said.* An excellent way of restating their thoughts is to start off by saying, "What I'm hearing you say is...."

By really listening, you can decipher the facts intelligently. Jumping in and interrupting puts your feelings in charge of your words. Practice patience and listen to the facts presented. It could be quite possible that they are correct in what they are presenting and you might be wrong. You could learn something new by listening to their facts. Spouting off is rude and makes you look foolish.

*Taken from *Devoted: God's Design for Marriage*, Copyright © 2016 by Dewey Wilson, Ph.D., Strong Marriages.

Intelligent people are always ready to learn, Their ears are open for knowledge.

— Proverbs 18:15

Better to remain silent and be thought a fool than to speak out and remove all doubt.

— Abraham Lincoln

A basic principle for making sound decisions involves listening to all the facts before answering. It can be difficult because you would like to get your point across as well. Listening to the facts requires calmly obtaining additional information and would keep you from judging too soon.

Husbands and wives will always have conflicts and disagreements. Breaking down the barriers to that communication block means listening effectively.

Ears to hear and eyes to see — both are gifts from the LORD.

— Proverbs 20:12

TAKE ACTION

- Practice saying, "What I'm hearing you say is..." to your spouse's statements during conversations. Then the other one should respond with, "Yes, what you heard me saying was correct" or with, "No, that is not exactly what I said," and then they should repeat their statement.

PRAY

Him: • Thank God for giving you two ears and one mouth as a reminder of the importance of listening.

Her: • Thank God for peace and listening skills in resolving conflicts.

KISSING HONESTLY

An honest answer is like a kiss on the lips.
— Proverbs 24:26 (NIV)

Is there not a more effective means of communication than a kiss? There are several forms — a kiss on the forehead, a kiss on the cheek, a kiss on the hand. But a kiss on the lips comprehensively says, "I love you." Everyone loves receiving a kiss from their lover.

Let him kiss me with the kisses of his mouth — For your love is better than wine.
— Song of Songs 1:2 (NKJV)

Honesty is likened to experiencing a wonderful expression of a kiss on the lips. Honest information needs to be expressed and received for the good of a marriage. Complaints must be heard and honored lovingly and graciously.

Certainly, no one would enjoy being kissed by lying lips. Dishonesty is inaccurate information and can leave a sour taste. Don't leave your spouse with a false impression about your thoughts, feelings, habits, likes, dislikes, personal history, daily activities, or future plans. Deliberately keeping personal information from your spouse is being dishonest. Dishonesty robs your spouse from being able to love you fully.

When it comes right down to it, simply telling the truth is easier than trying to keep lies straight.

The Lord detests lying lips, but he delights in those who tell the truth.
— Proverbs 12:22

A vital key in good communication is honesty. If what you're saying isn't true, then nothing real is being shared. Speak your truth, as much as you are able, with clarity, love and gentleness. When you communicate your truth from a place of love, you'll always be reinforcing the strength of your relationship. You have to be honest.

Honesty builds trust. Any form of deception is the biggest trust killer. Honesty will show your vulnerability. Being totally transparent in your relationship puts everything in the open. How can you be a team if you're not on the same page? In order to work together, you need to be upfront with one another. This way you can embrace each other and face life as one.

A maximum marriage has an open and connected dialogue. You are in control of the way you communicate with each other. Honesty will create unification, standing together as one, ready to face whatever life may hold. Honesty is a high form of intimacy — as pleasant as lip kissing.

The sound of a kiss is not so loud as that of a cannon, but its echo lasts a great deal longer.

— Oliver Wendell Holmes

TAKE ACTION

- Have you told white lies? Clear the air. Saying, "I'm sorry" can bring you closer than the dishonest deed that could drive you farther apart. It's communicating with grace.
- Kissing always bring you closer together, so kiss!

PRAY

Him: • Ask God to give you grace, gentleness, and honesty when communicating with your wife.

Her: • Thank God for loving, open and honest communication with your husband.

GUARDING YOUR SPEECH

Whoever guards his mouth and tongue keeps his soul from troubles.
— Proverbs 21:23 (NKJV) (See also Proverbs 13:3)

A person who is careful in what they say is wise. They think before speaking. They know when silence is best and they're the ones you'd most want to get advice from.

In a marriage, guarding what you say is critical. Harsh words cannot be taken back or erased. They hurt. And you have to live with the one you hurt. Careful words can actually keep us out of trouble, but careless words can cause trouble.

For we all stumble in many ways. And if anyone does not stumble in what he says, he is a perfect man, able also to bridle his whole body.
— James 3:2

James goes on to say in 3:3–13 you can bless or curse with your tongue and that the root of your mouth problem is a heart problem. What is in your heart will come out of your mouth. The solution to overcoming your heart problem is to give your heart fully to Jesus. Allowing Him to cleanse it will allow blessings of wisdom and kindness to proceed out of it. We have all said things that we wish we had not spoken. When this happens, the only way to make things right is to apologize and admit what we said was wrong. Even though this is hard, you'll earn respect.

Then the focus of your words should be ones that bless—words that are faith-filled. If you make an effort to bless with your words, what a difference you'll experience personally. Have you ever prayed a blessing over someone or given them encouragement such as the following verses?

May the Lord bless you and protect you. May the Lord smile on you and be gracious to you. May the Lord show you his favor and give you his peace.

— Numbers 6:24-26

This was a prayer in the Old Testament reserved for a priest. But 1 Peter 2:9 says we believers are "chosen as a royal priesthood." So, as a member of the royal priesthood, it is powerfully relevant how you use your words toward others. Your words should always bless others and build them up (Eph. 4:29b).

If someone ticks you off and your tendency is to say something harsh to them — or even silently to yourself about them — try asking God to protect them, to smile on them, to be gracious to them, and to give them peace. You could even mutter a quiet, "Bless their hearts."

An amazing transformation will result when you make an effort to pray a blessing over others. *You* will reap those blessings that you speak. I would certainly want God to smile over me and be gracious to me and to give me favor. And peace.

Careful (faith-filled) words put you in the position to receive all that God desires for you to have and become all that God desires for you to be. However, careless words may ruin everything. Be determined to speak kind, faith-filled words today!

TAKE ACTION

- Pray the blessing prayer mentioned above over your spouse substituting your spouse's name in place of the the word "you."

PRAY

Him: • Pray Psalm 51:10: "'Create in me a clean heart, O God. Renew a loyal spirit within me' so that my words would be a blessing to others."

Her: • Ask for forgiveness for the careless words you may have thrown about without thinking. Ask for a heart that produces words of wisdom and kindness.

BEING CONFIDENTIAL (GOSSIP, Part 1)

A gossip goes around telling secrets, but those who are trustworthy can keep a confidence.

— Proverbs 11:13

What I can always count on with my wife is that she is on my side. Regardless, I can take advantage of her like-mindedness. Sometimes when I'm upset and frustrated with someone, I'll come to her to vent, knowing she'll be confidential, and won't spread the ugly words to anyone else. She can be a sympathetic audience, unless I'm too mean-spirited. Then she will set me straight to try to understand the other person's standpoint.

You see, with her on my side, it can make my sin seem okay. The fact is, gossip is gossip. Neither of us should say harmful things about others. In reality, gossip in marriage can have two consequences:

> 1. Rather than sharpen, gossip dulls. Proverbs 27:17 tells us, "As iron sharpens iron, so one person sharpens another." Spouses who only stroke one another's egos, rather than push back in thoughtful conversation, are unlikely to grow. That is not to say that couples should indulge in conflict, but simply be wary of encouraging one another's [gripes about others].
>
> 2. Your marriage can become destructive. Couples who are mutually and dogmatically blind can act as a terrible force. These are the couples who partner with one another in dividing a church. These are the couples who discourage reconciliation when one or the other conflicts with a co-worker, family member, or neighbor. Rather than encourage civility and restoration, their marriage is a crucible of gossip, bitterness, anger, and self-righteousness, all melded together into impenetrable obstinacy.[1]

A gossip goes around telling secrets, so don't hang around with chatterers.

— Proverbs 20:19

Secrets about others. Secrets about ourselves. Confidentiality can be a tricky line. Charles Swindoll suggests you establish four practical ground rules when it comes to confidentiality:

1. Whatever you're told in confidence, do not repeat.
2. Whenever you're tempted to tell a secret, do not yield.
3. Whomever you're talking about, do not gossip.
4. However you're prone to disagree, do not slander.[2]

A confidence kept gives others confidence in you.
— Charles Swindoll

Left unchecked, gossip can grow like a cancer. When you gripe to each other about someone else, eventually you'll start griping to others about that person. It's ten times worse if it's your spouse you're griping about. Gossip does not honor God, and as Ephesians 5:4 tells us, it is "out of place." There is a place for venting and listening, but a maximum marriage does so in a manner oriented toward love and mutual growth. Praise others. Praise each other.

TAKE ACTION

- Try to see the perspectives of others that you may not necessarily agree with. Rather than putting them down, pray for them.
- As you give words of affirmation towards each other, affirm others in the same way. This will squelch any destructible gossip.

PRAY

Him: • Ask God to keep your mouth shut when you want to gripe about someone.

Her: • Ask God to make you a loving, kind and trustworthy wife as well as a friend to others. And to keep secrets from spreading like a wildfire.

1. "Gossip in Marriage: The Ugly Truth" by Sharon Hodde Miller, April 1, 2013, sheworships.com. © 2017 Sharon Hodde Miller.
2. insight.org

FORSAKING ALL OTHERS (GOSSIP, Part 2)

A troublemaker plants seeds of strife; gossip separates the best of friends.

— Proverbs 16:28 (See also Proverbs 18:19)

As you read in Part 1, it can be easy for a husband and wife to become a team of secret slander. Slander is character assassination, bad-mouthing, and malicious gossip — whether you're putting down others together, or telling someone else a complaint about your spouse.

Studies have shown that physically complaining rewires your brain to be depressed and anxious. If you continually focus on being critical with bad thoughts, it is easier for your brain to bring those things to the surface.

In their book, *Boundaries in Marriage*, authors Dr. Henry Cloud and Dr. John Townsend describe in more detail the exclusivity of marriage and how gossiping within it destroys the relationship:

> "Marriage is an exclusive club. Marriage is a two-person arrangement, leaving out all other parties. This is why wedding vows often include the phrase, 'forsaking all others.' Boundaries in marriage are meant to create a safe place for one's soul; third parties can become disruptive to this safety.
>
> "Our love often gets segmented into other places. This problem, called triangulation, is one of the great enemies of good marriages. Triangulation occurs when one spouse brings in a third party for an unhealthy reason. A 'triangle' is created when, for example, a wife (Person A) goes to a friend (Person C) for something that she should go to her husband (Person B) for. Here are some examples of triangulation that occur in marriage:
>
> - A wife talks to her best friend about her unhappiness with her husband, but doesn't let him know her feelings.
> - A husband confides to his secretary that his wife doesn't understand him.
> - One spouse makes their child a confidant, becoming closer to the child than to her mate.
> - A husband is more invested in his parents than in his wife.

> "In all these examples, a spouse is taking a part of his heart away from his mate and bringing it to an outside source. This is not only painful, but also unjust. It works against what God intended to develop in marriage—the mysterious unity that brings the couple closer to each other in ever-deepening ways. Triangulation betrays trust and fractures the union. Gossip is a form of triangulation."*

The one who conceals hatred has lying lips, and whoever utters slander is a fool.

— Proverbs 10:18 (ESV)

When Solomon says that gossip separates the best of friends, that should be the red flag to stay away from it! Why would you want to destroy your best friendship — your marriage? Never allow someone outside of your marriage to hear complaints about your spouse. And also complaining about others to each other should be done cautiously. You're playing with gossip fire.

Pay attention to the words you speak. It is possible to rewire your brain to think good thoughts and pleasant things about others. The maximum marriage will thrive through this daily practice.

TAKE ACTION

- Tell each other 3 things that you like about the other.
- Tell each other some good traits about someone you may not get along with. This will be hard, but it's the rewiring of your thought pattern to think more Christ-like.

PRAY

Him: • Ask God for the confidence to see the good in others, especially your wife; to be more Christ-like in your words.

Her: • Ask God to give you a mentality of positivity and to forsake all others that might breed negative thoughts.

---

* *Boundaries in Marriage* Copyright ©1999 by Henry Cloud and John Townsend, Zondervan Publishers, Grand Rapids, MI

UNPACKING GRACE, Part 1

Though He scoffs at the scoffers and scorns the scorners, Yet He gives His grace [His undeserved favor] to the humble [those who give up self-importance].

— Proverbs 3:34 (AMP) (See also James 4:6)

"For by grace you have been saved through faith. And this is not your own doing; it is the gift of God, not a result of works, so that no one may boast" (Eph. 2:8–9 ESV). *Grace.* It's the only way we'll ever see Heaven. Notice how the Amplified Version of today's Proverb defines grace: His undeserved favor. And Paul adds that it's a gift.

Your marriage should be overflowing with grace — God's grace to you and your grace to your spouse. You can gift your spouse with graciousness just as God has gifted you. Here are four practical expectations you can receive by unpacking grace.

1. **You can expect to gain a greater appreciation for God's gifts to you and others.** What are your gifts? Your salvation is a gift. Your life is a gift. There's also the gifts of laughter, music, beauty, friendship, and forgiveness. Share them with others.

2. **You can expect to spend less time and energy critical of and concerned about others' choices.** Wouldn't that be a refreshing relief? When you get a grasp on grace — when you begin to operate in a context of freedom — you become increasingly less petty. You will allow others room to make their own decisions in life, even though you may choose otherwise. What peace that will bring to a marriage!

3. **You can expect to become more tolerant and less judgmental.** Externals will not mean as much to you. You'll begin to cultivate a desire for authentic faith rather than endure a religion based on superficial performance. You will find yourself so involved in your own pursuit of grace, you'll no longer lay guilt trips on those with whom you disagree. Because God has given you His gift of grace when you least deserved it, you can demonstrate it willingly to others.

4. **You can expect to take a giant step toward maturity.**

> As your world expands, thanks to an awakening of your understanding of grace, your maturity will enlarge. Before your very eyes, new vistas will open. It will be so transforming, you will never be the same. When you truly realize what God has done for you, His love, grace and forgiveness begin to transform every area of your life.*

Grace means undeserved kindness. It is the gift of God to man the moment he sees he is unworthy of God's favor.

— Dwight L. Moody

Grace, it is sovereign, it is free, it is sure, it is unconditional, and it is everlasting.

— Alexander Whyte

Imperfection is the prerequisite for grace. Light only gets in through the cracks.

— Philip Yancey

You can't earn grace by trying to be good. Grace is unconditional. The same concept makes a maximum marriage. The love you demonstrate towards your spouse is to be unconditional. Their imperfections are to be covered with your grace.

TAKE ACTION

- An acronym for GRACE is: **G**od's **R**iches **A**t **C**hrist's **E**xpense. Think about how rich you are because you've been gifted with grace through the redemptive love of Christ.

PRAY

Him: • Thank God for His amazing grace.
Her: • Thank God for His unconditional love.

---

*Taken from *The Grace Awakening* by Charles R. Swindoll. Copyright © 1990, 1996, 2003 by Charles R. Swindoll, Inc. Thomas Nelson, Nashville, TN

UNPACKING GRACE, Part 2

One who loves a pure heart and who speaks with grace will have the king for a friend.

— Proverbs 22:11 (NIV)

In 1936, Dale Carnegie wrote the book, *How to Win Friends and Influence People*, which has sold more than 15 million copies worldwide. Here, Solomon shows us how to win friends in one word — grace. Especially winning those friends in high places. Your spouse is your highest priority friend on earth (see page 98), so it makes sense to communicate grace to them. Let's look at how that can be accomplished.

- **Show grace with words.** "Let your conversation be gracious and attractive so that you will have the right response for everyone" (Col. 4:5).
- **Show grace with kindness.** "Now then, please…show kindness to my family, because I have shown kindness to you" (Josh. 2:12 NIV).
- **Show grace with gratefulness.** "Let the message of Christ dwell among you richly as you teach and admonish one another with all wisdom…singing to God with gratitude in your hearts" (Col. 3:16 NIV).
- **Show grace with humility.** "Don't be selfish; don't try to impress others. Be humble, thinking of others as better than yourselves" (Phil. 2:3).
- **Show grace with love.** "Let's not merely say that we love each other; let us show the truth by our actions" (1 John 3:18).
- **Show grace with sincerity.** "Don't look out only for your own interests, but take an interest in others, too" (Phil. 2:4).

[God] said, "My grace is all you need. My power works best in weakness." So now I am glad to boast about my weaknesses, so that the power of Christ can work through me.

— 2 Corinthians 12:9

Marvelous, infinite, matchless grace,
Freely bestowed on all who believe!
— Hymn "Grace Greater Than Our Sin" written by Julia H. Johnston, 1910

You demonstrate grace by your loving actions toward others. Wouldn't you want to be a spouse with the personality of pureness of heart and gracious speech? Think of how refreshing it is to be around such a person. Such a person communicates grace. Such a person is attractive. Such a person will always have friends — even friends of high magnitude.

Do you want to win friends and influence people? Reach out to others with grace and God will give you the rewards of doing so. It may not be natural for you to show grace to everyone (especially difficult people), but when you do, it brings glory to God because you're imitating Him.

Each of you should use whatever gift you have received to serve others, as faithful stewards of God's grace in its various forms.
— 1 Peter 4:10 (NIV)

TAKE ACTION

- Practice the 6 ways to show grace this week. Concentrate on one each day.

PRAY

Him: • Pray 2 Corinthians 9:15.

Her: • Pray Psalm 136:1. Thank Him for His loving, saving, and matchless grace!

EARNING RESPECT

People with integrity walk safely, but those who follow crooked paths will be exposed.

— Proverbs 10:9

Aretha Franklin, the queen of R&B music, had a very popular song in 1967 called "Respect." It's catchy tune went, "R-E-S-P-E-C-T. Find out what it means to me." We all want a little respect, don't we? We all want people to admire us for who we are, prompted by our abilities, qualities, or achievements.

If anyone knew about respect, it was certainly Solomon. He was one of the most highly respected men in the world. But respect isn't something that you get automatically. It has to be earned. Solomon reveals to us habits we have to cultivate in order to earn respect. One is speaking with integrity and walking in integrity.

Here are three ways to earn respect. First, if you want others to look up to you, speak truthfully and be dependable. No one admires someone who says they are going to do something and then fails to deliver what they promised. Someone who has the traits of integrity, honor, decency and trustworthiness are held in the highest regard.

The integrity of the upright guides them, but the unfaithful are destroyed by their duplicity.

— Proverbs 11:3

The second way to earn respect is to live a godly life. Proverbs 11:27 states: "If you search for good, you will find favor...." In the previous verses of the 11th chapter, *good* is defined as mercy, not cruelty (v. 17); righteousness, not wickedness (v. 18); and doing what pleases God (v. 20). *Favor* is the blessing and respect of people. Do you want respect? Seek goodness, and kindness will be returned to you.

The third way to earn respect is to walk in humility.

Pride ends in humiliation, while humility brings honor.

— Proverbs 29:23

Having a humble spirit gains respect. Not so with those who are arrogant. People will respect a person who realizes he can't really take the credit for any of his accomplishments. They understand their skills are given to them by God.

Fire tests the purity of silver and gold, but a person is tested by being praised.

— Proverbs 27:21

When someone praises you for an accomplishment, does it go to your head? Do you brag about your abilities? I have a friend, and whenever I compliment him on a job well done, he says, "Praise God." He always gives God the credit. That's humility!

A strong marriage is one where the husband and wife each speak truthfully, seek godliness, and are humble. They deliberately make efforts to earn respect. In doing so, they walk safely in integrity.

▩ TAKE ACTION

- Look at yourself and see if you can see the traits of integrity, honor, decency and trustworthiness in your own lifestyle.

▩ PRAY

Him:
- Ask God for integrity in your speech and in your walk.
- Thank God for His goodness and favor.

Her:
- Ask God to give you the ability to walk humbly. It's hard.
- Praise God for your skills and accomplishments.

SHOWING RESPECT

Give her credit for all she does. She deserves the respect of everyone.
— Proverbs 31:31 (GNT)

The Proverbs 31 wife is one who has earned respect. When you treat others with respect, it shows that you recognize their value and worth. Respect is important in any relationship. For a relationship to be successful, there has to be great respect for one another, even when disagreements arise. (See more on Proverbs 31 on pages 214–223)

It has been said that women need love while men need respect. While this may be psychologically true, everyone needs both love and respect. Everyone wants to feel valued. I'm not going to expound on husbands as the only one who need respect. 1 Peter 2:17 says, "Show proper respect to everyone" (NIV). 1 Peter 3:7 tells us, "Husbands… be considerate as you live with your wives, and treat them with respect…"(NIV). And Ephesians 5:33, "…Let the wife see that she respects her husband" (NKJV). Showing respect honors God.

Sometimes it can be hard to show respect. But since God has commanded in these verses that you show respect to your spouse, you should never use the excuse that they haven't earned your respect. Everyone is imperfect. Be careful not to let their failures erode your respect for their good qualities. Their value should never be based on performance.

Check out these qualities that grow from showing respect.

- Respect improves trust.
- Respect increases confidence in the other.
- Respect acknowledges potential.
- Respect provides encouragement.
- Being respected improves the ability to love.
- Being respected reduces the fear of failure or feeling inadequate.

Here are five ways to show gratitude and respect for your spouse.

1. Listen. International best-selling author Bryant H. McGill says, "One of the most sincere forms of respect is actually listening to what another has to say." Make eye contact. Everyone loves the person who shows a genuine interest in what they have to say.

2. Encourage. Dale Carnegie said, "Perhaps you will forget tomorrow the kind words you say today, but the recipient may cherish them over a lifetime." Taking an interest in another's feelings and giving them an uplifting word can truly brighten their day.

3. Congratulate. Give credit and acknowledgment of a job well done. Express praise and gratitude when it's deserved. You can find good in anyone if you look hard enough. It really comes down to appreciation.

4. Be Helpful. Do a good deed by providing favors for someone in any way that you can. Acts of kindness can do wonders.

5. Say, "Thank You." This may seem like common sense but can easily be forgotten. People love to be appreciated for their actions.

Marriages between presumably incompatible people with a mutual respect can far outlast "perfect couple" marriages who never learned to appreciate each other. Opportunities to thank and compliment spouses can be taken for granted. Take time to show your appreciation and gratitude. Not only does it make your spouse feel better, but you will feel uplifted as well. For a maximum marriage, remember two basic guidelines for success: mutual respect and gratitude.

TAKE ACTION

- Talk about how being respected makes you feel.
- Show respect to each other by saying, "Please" and "Thank you" even if it seems trivial.

PRAY

Him: • Ask God to give you the skills of handing out respect.
• Thank God for your wife and her abilities.

Her: • Give God gratitude for your husband.

HONORED TO BE SECOND

Haughtiness goes before destruction; humility precedes honor.
— Proverbs 18:12 (See also Proverbs 11:2; 16:18; 15:33)

Perhaps you've heard the saying, "Pride goes before a fall." People who say this are actually quoting a paraphrase of Proverbs 16:18 and 18:12. We don't use the word "haughty" much. But it means the same as pride, arrogance, vain, conceitedness, a pompous attitude. Having these characteristics will only bring you ruin.

C. H. Spurgeon put it this way: "When men have ridden the high horse, destruction has always overtaken them. Let David's aching heart show that there is an eclipse of a man's glory when he dotes upon his own greatness (2 Sam. 24:10). See Nebuchadnezzar, the mighty builder of Babylon, creeping on the earth, devouring grass like oxen, until his nails had grown like bird's claws, and his hair like eagle's feathers (Dan. 4:33). Pride made the boaster a beast, as once before it made an angel a devil. God hates high looks, and never fails to bring them down. There is no wisdom in self-exaltation." (See also page 14 on Pride)

The opposite of pride is humility. Spurgeon goes on to say, "It is not humility to underrate yourself. Humility is to think of yourself, if you can, as God thinks of you." It doesn't mean to have a low self-esteem or a lack of confidence. God thinks highly of you and you should too.

Humility is not thinking less of yourself, it's thinking of yourself less.
— C. S. Lewis

Timothy Keller says, "The Christian Gospel is that I am so flawed that Jesus had to die for me, yet I am so loved and valued that Jesus was glad to die for me. This leads to deep humility and deep confidence at the same time. It undermines both swaggering and sniveling. I cannot feel superior to anyone, and yet I have nothing to prove to anyone. I do not think more of myself, nor less of myself. Instead, I think of myself less." In his book *Humility*, first published in 1895, Andrew Murray wrote, "Here is the path to the higher life: down, lower down! Just as water always seeks and fills the lowest place, so the moment God finds men abased and empty, His glory and power flow in to exalt and to bless."

Humility is royalty without a crown.
— Spencer W. Kimball

Jesus Christ was the perfect life-example of humility. When he stooped to wash the disciples' feet (John 13:1–17), he showed how an attitude of servant-hood leads to greatness. When you seek supremacy, you displease the Lord who promised that true greatness in His kingdom is attained by those with a servant's heart (Mark 9:35; 10:44). When you have a true servant's heart, the Lord promised you will be greatly blessed (John 13:17).

The maximum marriage knows that humility leads the way to honor. Serving one another is your role. Put the other above you in first place. If you want destruction, be haughty; if you want honor, show humility and be second.

TAKE ACTION

- Have you ever washed your spouse's feet? Do something today that will make your spouse drop their jaw in gratitude.

PRAY

Him:
- Ask God for forgiveness when you've been prideful.
- Ask God to destroy pride in your lifestyle so as not to bring destruction.

Her:
- Ask God for a humble attitude.
- Thank God for the life-example of Jesus.

STIRRING UP PROSPERITY

He who is of a proud heart stirs up strife, But he who trusts in the LORD will be prospered.

— Proverbs 28:25 (NKJV)

I believe the number one reason for any destroyed marriage is selfishness. One or both people in the marriage are only looking out for their own interests. Pride and selfishness are not taught to us, they're embedded within everyone of us from birth. Parents don't have to teach their youngster to be selfish — the child will inevitably hoard their own toys or cry for food whenever they want to. Selfishness is all around us. It's a "me, me, me" world. "Always looking out for number one." This only leads to discord. Read Paul's warning:

Don't be selfish; don't try to impress others. Be humble, thinking of others as better than yourselves. Don't look out only for your own interests, but take an interest in others, too.

— Philippians 2:3–4

Eugene Patterson's expression of this verse from Philippians in *The Message* reads, "Don't push your way to the front; don't sweet-talk your way to the top. Put yourself aside, and help others get ahead. Don't be obsessed with getting your own advantage. Forget yourselves long enough to lend a helping hand." Do you realize what would happen if everyone lived this way? There would be no wars. There would be less crime. Everyone would get along with each other. The world would be much more peaceful.

How can you achieve this seemingly unattainable tranquility? Paul answers that for us in Phil. 2:5, "You must have the same attitude that Christ Jesus had." The following verses explain that attitude. Although Jesus was equal with God, he did not exalt himself nor demand an exalted position. He willingly lowered himself to human form, he humbled himself in obedience to God. Verse 9 states, "Therefore, God elevated him to the place of highest honor and gave him the name above all other names."

> To light the spark and begin to desire to lay down our own rights and privileges and lift up the rights of others, we must understand the concept of the Cross. Having an attitude of humility requires we understand we are only able to stand before God because of the price Jesus has paid. We draw each breath only as God gives it to us, only because of His abundant grace. How could we even think of being conceited when we realize we owe the very breath we draw to Jesus Christ?*

O people, the Lord has told you what is good, and this is what he requires of you: to do what is right, to love mercy, and to walk humbly with your God.

— Micah 6:8

Perfect marriage advice for a maximum relationship: trust in the Lord and walk humbly with Him. The opposite attitude, thinking only about yourself, stirs up dissension. Humility stirs up prosperity.

TAKE ACTION

- Look hard at your own desires and wants in your relationship. Are they "me-centered"? Choose to pursue prosperity. Choose to put the other's needs above your own.
- Make Micah 6:8 your quest today.

PRAY

Him:
- Thank Jesus for his exceedingly abundance of humility.
- Ask God to empower you to overcome selfishness.

Her:
- Thank God for every breath you take and for His grace.
- Ask God to empower you to overcome selfishness.

**The Swindoll Study Bible,* p. 1489, Charles R. Swindoll, Tyndale House Publishers, Inc.

REAPING A REWARD, Part 1

Everyone who is proud and arrogant in heart is disgusting and exceedingly offensive to the LORD*; Be assured he will not go unpunished.*
— Proverbs 16:5 (AMP)

I've come to realize that an arrogant person can never be happy. I know because I have personally walked that road. Arrogance grows from being prideful. Just because you believe you're something special doesn't mean you are. In fact, you're not. I came to grips with my attitude when I realized how unhappy I was. I believe it was God reprimanding me. I needed to learn how to be humble. Pride is about my glory; humility is about God's glory.

If you have been a fool by being proud…, cover your mouth in shame.
— Proverbs 30:32

This is a real gut-puncher. Who in their right mind would want to disgust and offend God? I would want to please Him and make Him smile. I would want to reap God's blessings on my life. Solomon shares this hope:

The LORD *mocks the mockers but is gracious to the humble.*
— Proverbs 3:34

Proverbs 3:34 is quoted twice in the New Testament — 1 Peter 5:5 and James 4:6. When Peter and James quoted it, they used a Greek translation of the Old Testament, and so it is quoted as, "God opposes the proud but gives grace to the humble."

It all begins with God. Notice how the verse starts, "God…." If you want to be humble in this life, like this Proverb, you must remember everything starts with God. Peter and James set the context of our reality. You don't live in a universe that revolves around you. You don't live in a world that you created. You don't live in a world where God is absent and not running the show. God is to be first in your life. In your marriage. In your job. In everything.

God is gracious to the humble. He gives us grace. What a promise! Grace is the very thing that makes relationships thrive. The ESV translation says God gives favor to the humble. Put the following verse in the context of your marriage:

If my people, who are called by my name, will humble themselves and pray and seek my face and turn from their wicked ways, then I will hear from heaven, and I will forgive their sin and will heal their land.

— 2 Chronicles 7:14 (NIV)

For a marriage to be ever-thriving, the husband and wife will humble themselves, pray and seek God, and turn from wickedness. Arrogance is wicked. God will bless the humble couple and give them grace and favor. A fulfilling life starts with the Lord's favor.

Be completely humble and gentle; be patient, bearing with one another in love.

— Ephesians 4:2 (NIV)

TAKE ACTION

- Humble yourself. Pray. Seek God. Turn from wrongdoing. Wait for God's reward.

PRAY

Him: • Pray Psalm 90:17 (ESV), "Let the favor of the Lord our God be upon us, and establish the work of our hands upon us; yes, establish the work of our hands!"

Her: • Ask God to help you gain a heart of wisdom into His humility by getting the proper perspective on who you are compared to who He is.

REAPING A REWARD, Part 2

The reward for humility and fear of the LORD *is riches and honor and life.*
— Proverbs 22:4 (ESV)

Blessings follow obedience (see page 184). Here Solomon gives us *two* prerequisites for *three* blessings. I think that's a good deal!

Humility is the first requirement. It is lived out by taking correction, saying you are sorry, avoiding public praise, serving others quietly, being reserved publicly, never talking about yourself, and praising others.

The fear of the Lord is the other condition (see 10). This is reverently seeking to honor God in all you do. This person avoids anything to dishonor God as much as possible. He or she longs to hear God through His Word, loves what God loves and hates what He hates. (see pages 14–17; Prov. 8:13).

Once these two conditions are met, the blessings will flow. Riches are the first blessing. This could mean wealth, but money isn't everything. Proverbs 16:8 says, "Better to have little, with godliness, than to be rich and dishonest." Riches can also mean spiritual blessings. If you are discontent with what God has given you, you don't have humility or fear of the Lord.

The second blessing is honor. A humble person who fears the Lord will grow in favor with God and men. Remember Proverbs 18:12, "Humility precedes honor." The almighty God honors those who honor Him. A man who fears the Lord is filled with God's grace and will be honored by others.

Life is the third blessing. The word "life" means things that cannot be described here on earth. "Eye has not seen, nor ear heard, nor have entered into the heart of man the things which God has prepared for those who love Him" (1 Corinthians 2:9). Yet Scripture does mention you can have an abundant life, a good life, a joyful life, a peaceful life, a productive life, an extended life, and eternal life. All for here on earth and eternity.

He leads the humble in doing right, teaching them His way.
— Psalm 25:9

There is no shortcut to achieve humility and the fear of the Lord. The requirements must be exercised as the necessary conditions to reach prosperity and success.

Pride must die in you, or nothing of heaven can live in you.
— Andrew Murray, *Humility*

One the best-loved Psalms is the 23rd. It is a great illustration of humility. It is written from the viewpoint of a sheep. Throughout the Bible, God's people are depicted as these lowly creatures under the care of their Shepherd. The first verse of this Psalm states the entire theme: "The Lord is my shepherd; I have all that I need." After listing all the gifts the Lord provides, the psalmist states that God's goodness and unfailing love will pursue him all of his life.

Psalm 131 is another psalm of humility. The first verse states the theme by not being proud or haughty. Then the remaining verses move into the description of contentment through quietness, calmness, and peacefulness.

Coming before God with humility and awe reaps the rewards of riches, honor and life. It doesn't get much better than that!

TAKE ACTION

- Read Psalm 23 and 131 and reflect on how they show humility and the rewards of living a humble lifestyle.

PRAY

Him: • Pray Psalm 23.
Her: • Pray Psalm 131.

LIVING HUMBLY THROUGH MISSIONS

Better to live humbly with the poor than to share plunder with the proud.
— Proverbs 16:19

It is my strong belief that mission trips are an excellent way to completely understand the concept of humility. Missionaries who make their livelihood serving in this manner, as well as anyone who has been on a mission trip, can tell you awesome testimonies of how God works when you practice The Great Commission to tell others of Jesus. Humbly serving God puts it all into perspective of what life's purpose is for.

Here are 7 reasons compiled by J. Lee Grady on why you should seriously consider going on a mission trip if you haven't already.

> **1. You will encounter God's heart.** Our God is big and He cares about the nations. When you step into a foreign mission field, you will sense God's amazing compassion for another culture and you will begin to know Him as Lord of the harvest.
>
> **2. You will expand your limited perspective.** Too many of us are stuck in spiritual ruts. Expect to learn spiritually from the people you are going to minister to.
>
> **3. You will become more grateful.** I receive an attitude adjustment every time I go to another country. I come back from my trips with a renewed appreciation for life's little blessings—air conditioning, running water, nice roads and flush toilets. There's nothing like spending time with a family of seven in a house made of mud and straw to put your puny problems in perspective.
>
> **4. You will discover your spiritual family.** When you minister alongside Christians in another country, you find that the Holy Spirit bonds you together supernaturally. These relationships can last a lifetime. This is the same type of bond the apostle Paul felt with the people he met in Greece, Italy and Asia Minor during his travels.
>
> **5. You will build lasting partnerships.** God gives us this strong bond so we will link arms and work for a common purpose across racial and cultural lines.
>
> **6. You will overcome your fears.** [I've seen people who

feel inadequate spiritually] have more spiritual confidence when they get back home. Sometimes you have to run to the front of the battle line to get new courage.

7. You will expand the kingdom of Jesus. The Great Commission was not a suggestion. Christ's kingdom cannot be built without bold, radical obedience to Matthew 28:19: "Go therefore..." Somebody has to GO. There's no way around it. To share the gospel with the whole world, we must be willing to pack our bags sometime and leave home.*

One's pride will bring him low, but he who is lowly in spirit will obtain honor.

— Proverbs 29:23 (ESV)

Better to be a nobody and yet have a servant than pretend to be somebody and have no food.

— Proverbs 12:9 (NIV)

Having a maximum marriage is one where the husband and wife serve humbly — serving the poor as well as each other. You are no doubt blessed by God with many riches. Humble yourselves and thank Him by telling others about Him.

TAKE ACTION

- Look at the 7 reasons to go on a mission trip in perspective of your marriage relationship. Serving God within the context of The Great Commission will improve your relationship with God and each other.

PRAY

Together: • Seriously pray about going on a mission trip together. Ask God to provide the finances and time.

*Taken from "7 Reasons You Should Go on a Short-Term Mission Trip" by J. Lee Grady, former editor of *Charisma*. Copyright © 2019 Charisma Media

BECOMING DEVOTED FRIENDS

There are "friends" who destroy each other, but a real friend sticks closer than a brother.

— Proverbs 18:24

There are many types of friends: the occasional friend; the long-term friend; the one you're close to but they're not considered part of your inner circle; and those few who are members of your inner circle — a best friend. Obviously, you and your spouse started out as friends before you married. I believe your spouse can be your best friend, but you can also have a best friend outside of your marriage (as long as they're the same sex as you). In order to achieve a maximum marriage that is unified, husbands and wives have to be close, true, and faithful friends. Marriage without friendship cannot work.

For clarification in our study, I'm going to refer to the husband-wife team who nurture a "best friends" relationship as devoted friends. They are intimate, close-knit, tight-knit, inseparable, attached, and faithful. In fact, the word "sticks" in this Proverb is the same word used in Genesis 2:24 for "cleave:" "Therefore shall a man leave his father and his mother, and shall *cleave* unto his wife: and they shall be one flesh" (KJV). Cleaving, or sticking to, is a commitment to the permanency of marriage — to be super-glued together for life.

When difficulties come into a marriage, the devoted couple is just that — devoted. They stick with it and work through the difficulty together, as a team, for the good of their relationship. A devoted, maximum marriage is forged in the fires of adversity, all for the value of friendship.

The word "friendship" conjures up thoughts of honesty, vulnerability, companionship, and mutual respect. It also implies a certain outlaying of time and energy. C. S. Lewis said of friendship: "It is when we are doing things together that friendship springs up. Friends look in the same direction." The word *friend* is of Germanic origin meaning "to love."

A friend is always loyal, and a brother is born to help in time of need.
— Proverbs 17:17

The devoted couple spend time together, work together in raising the children, and keep no secrets between them. They are equally invested partners in the relationship. They make a point to concentrate on nurturing the friendship aspect. If the priority in your life becomes your career, your children, or a hobby, then your friendship with your spouse will run the risk of dying.

A maximum marriage is demonstrated in the following realities:

1. Embrace Jesus Christ as your first *spiritual* priority — love and obey Him. He is your ultimate devoted friend.
2. Make your spouse your number one *earthly* priority.

There is no greater love than to lay down one's life for one's friends. You are my friends if you do what I command....
— John 15:13–14

TAKE ACTION

- Set up a regular "date night" and stick to it.
- Pick a new hobby to learn together, or plan a vacation together.

PRAY

Him: • Ask God to make your friendship closer and more devoted.
• Thank God that you are a friendship team.

Her: • Ask God to help you build a true, intimate friendship.
• Thank God for your devoted husband.

ASSOCIATING WITH OTHER STRONG MARRIAGES

Walk with the wise and become wise; associate with fools and get in trouble.

— Proverbs 13:20

Great marriages are contagious! If you want a great marriage, surround yourself with couples who have one. Have you ever heard the saying, "If you want to soar with the eagles, you can't surround yourself with turkeys"?

It's important to have married friends who build you up and have admirable qualities in their own marriage. You grow spiritually by associating with friends who encourage you in your pursuit of godly wisdom by offering their own, or even showing you by example.

According to research done by professors Nicholas Christakis, Rose McDermott and James Fowler at the University of California in 2010, being friends with someone who gets divorced makes someone 147% more likely to get divorced themselves. People who are negative about, or failing at, marriage will have an impact on you.

George Washington said, "Associate yourself with men of good quality if you esteem your own reputation. It is better to be alone than in bad company."

...Bad company corrupts good character.

— 1 Corinthians 15:33

Don't befriend angry people or associate with hot-tempered people, or you will learn to be like them and endanger your soul.

— Proverbs 22:24–25

"Show me your friends and I'll show you your future," says Dr. Mark Ambrose, Executive Pastor of Pacific Coast Church in San Clemente, California. Motivational speaker Jim Rohn says, "You become like the five people you spend the most time with. Choose carefully."

Follow the steps of good men…
— Proverbs 2:20

You are the sum of who you spend your time with. Make sure that you are directly involved with people who lift you, inspire you, and motivate you to achieve more. If you have friends that might compromise your Christian character, think long and hard about even befriending them. A maximum marriage is continually growing, and this might mean changing friends who pull you down. That'll be for your own good.

Friendship is a sheltering tree.
— Samuel Taylor Coleridge, 19th-century English poet

When the heat of adversity comes your way, there is nothing quite like a sheltering tree for cool relief. Cultivate trees of friendships. Associate with friends who believe in you and in marriage itself. It's a wise choice for a maximum marriage!

TAKE ACTION

- Go out on a double date with another couple whose marriage you admire.
- Invite another couple or two over for a dinner and play some games.

PRAY

Him:
- Ask God to help you choose your married friends wisely.
- Thank God for the positive, encouraging friends you do have.

Her:
- Ask God to surround you with positive and godly women.
- Praise God for your admirable friends.

SHARPENING EACH OTHER

As iron sharpens iron, so a friend sharpens a friend.
— Proverbs 27:17

Devoted couples inspire each other, encourage each other, and bring out the best in each other. They are equally dedicated to improving the well-being of the relationship.

Devoted couples are able to acknowledge even their differences, and find a way to resolve them. As they do this, each one's character is refined, just as an iron blade is sharpened by the honing from another piece of iron. Even though sparks may fly when this happens, the end result is a sharpened edge.

If you're honest you'll admit you have some rough edges that need smoothing, polishing, and sharpening. Yet in terms of metal working, this is not the gentlest of processes. You might cringe at the sound of metal scraping on metal. You may be comfortable with your rough edges and may not always be eager to let them go. To lose your jagged edges, you must have a willing spirit that is open to being taught. It is crucial to accept your spouse's lovingly challenges of becoming more polished.

There is an important thing to remember here, however. You sharpen iron with iron. Iron cannot sharpen itself. Nor can something weaker than iron sharpen iron. The one who sharpens must be strong and refined themselves.

Be careful in understanding this doesn't mean trying to change him or her to become more like you. You cannot change your spouse's personality any more than you can change the color of their eyes. There shouldn't be any lecturing or manipulating. Consider the following actions you can take to point your spouse towards becoming more of the person God wants them to be.

- **Be patient and loving in your words.** Don't try to play God. Allow Him to be the ultimate Sharpener.

- **Don't stand in the way.** Remember, perfection isn't possible as you sharpen each other. Allow them some space and time to grow.
- **Be authentic.** Nobody wants to be smothered or judged or patronized. It's not about authority. Be transparent in showing that you need sharpening also from time to time.
- **Stay balanced.** Keep Jesus at the center of your relationship. Remember, you're friends. Having a "holier than thou" attitude will do more harm and hinder your sharpening ability.

The maximum marriage has two people who are true friends who build each other up spiritually. The husband should show Jesus to his wife. The wife should show Jesus to the husband. Jesus is the third strand in a triple-braided maximum marriage.

Two people are better off than one, for they can help each other succeed. If one person falls, the other can reach out and help. But someone who falls alone is in real trouble. Likewise, two people lying close together can keep each other warm. But how can one be warm alone? A person standing alone can be attacked and defeated, but two can stand back-to-back and conquer. Three are even better, for a triple-braided cord is not easily broken.

— Ecclesiastes 4:9–12

TAKE ACTION

- Ask the other how you need to be polished and sharpened.

PRAY

Him:
- Thank God for your wifely friend who sharpens you.
- Thank Him for being the third strand in your marriage.

Her:
- Thank God for the support of your loving husband.
- Thank Him for being the third strand in your marriage.

MENDING THE FLAWS

The heartfelt counsel of a friend is as sweet as perfume and incense.
— Proverbs 27:9

You typically don't think of criticism as being a good thing. It definitely means finding fault and exposing it. But it is possible to learn from criticism, especially from one whom is closest to you, your spouse. There are times when a word of criticism can be a helpful factor in your character and spiritual growth.

A marriage based on solid friendship is not threatened by honest criticism. Rather, it is strengthened. I could be the world's champion at saying wrong things. And I've learned this over the years by the scars and bruises I've received by kicks to my shins under the table. Truthfully, those actions were a wake-up call that I let some words slip out of my mouth that I shouldn't have. My wife is less abusive nowadays — instead, I'll get the "look."

I've learned to be more careful in what I say now to others as well as to her. Later, after we've been in a gathering of our group of friends, I can ask her if there was anything I said that could have hurt or offended someone. I can be certain she will let me honestly know.

An open rebuke is better than hidden love! Wounds from a sincere friend are better than many kisses from an enemy.
— Proverbs 27:5–6

Notice how Solomon says in the above Proverb it's a *sincere* friend. One who is close to you. One who knows you profoundly. Criticism may wound, but wounds can heal. We all need that close friend who will stab us in the front — to hit us where we need to be hit.

So what about criticism from others — those kisses from an enemy? You can take a lesson from Nehemiah 2:19–20 and 4:1–5. The story describes how Nehemiah faced open criticism, false accusations, and gross misunderstanding in his quest to rebuild the wall around his hometown of Jerusalem. In spite of the obstacles and critics, he kept his cool. He stayed in the race. He refused to get discouraged. He went to God in prayer. And he built the wall.

When you are criticized by those who don't know you well, filter out what is actual truth and ignore all the rest. Nehemiah sought God's wisdom through prayer giving him thorough confidence in achieving the task.

He has a right to criticize, who has a heart to help.
— Abraham Lincoln

Heartfelt counsel is sweet. Your spouse has a heart for you. Of course you both should be careful not to be over critical of each other to spoil the sweetness. You can help mend the shortcomings of the other with proper, heartfelt words. Never nag or attack to hurt. Don't put them on the defensive by saying, "You are always ________," or "You never ____________." Begin your statements with, "I feel like ______," or "I felt hurt by ___________." Two loving people look after each other and the friendship grows.

TAKE ACTION

- Clear the air with each other if hurtful, critical comments have been made in the past and ask forgiveness. Seek ways to counsel each other with sweet words.

PRAY

Him:
- Praise God for your loving wife who wants you to grow in character and spirit.
- Ask God to give you wisdom in counseling her lovingly.

Her:
- Ask God to give you a vocabulary of sweetness whenever you need to confront your husband about his less-than-desirable actions.

BEING LOYAL, Part 1

A friend is always loyal, and a brother is born to help in time of need.
— Proverbs 17:17

Have you ever thought about how God mapped out your entire life when you were still in the womb? (Psalm 139:16) Consider the situation that in another part of your city, state, country, or world — at another time — your spouse was born as part of His plan for your life. God brought the two of you together to complete His purpose. Comprehend that amazing fact and you'll realize how important commitment is in your marriage.

Your spouse was designed by the Creator just for you! Think back on how you met. God brought those circumstances together so that you would meet up, fall in love, and then marry. Even if you met on-line, God orchestrated it. What God brings together, no one should ever separate (Mark 10:9).

So God tells you to be supportive and to encourage each other. Your closest human relationship is to be to your personally-designed spouse. It is to be true friendship. You are to be supportive, encouraging, forgiving, and loving to each other always. This paints a clear picture of exactly how God is toward us — supportive, encouraging, forgiving, and loving.

God's love never ends and He will never fail you or abandon you (Deuteronomy 31:6, 8; Hebrews 13:5). God is committed to you. Even when you mess up, He still loves you. It's how you should commit to your spouse. The English Standard Version of this verse in Proverbs says, "A friend loves at all times." It doesn't say some of the time, or most of the time, or only if you don't mess up—it's *all* the time.

If a friend is to be always loyal, then certainly you, as a spouse, should be also. And if a true friend is born to help in time of need, then it makes sense that God created your spouse to help you through adversity and hardships in your life. You need each other.

[9]Two people are better off than one, for they can help each other succeed. [10]If one person falls, the other can reach out and help. But someone who falls alone is in real trouble. [11]Likewise, two people lying close together can keep each other warm. But how can one be warm alone? [12]A person standing alone can be attacked and defeated, but two can stand back-to-back and conquer. Three are even better, for a triple-braided cord is not easily broken.

— Ecclesiastes 4:9–12

The qualities of a true spouse are best exemplified in the life of our Lord. Jesus reminded us that the greatest of all love is expressed when a friend is prepared to give up his own life for that of his friend — or to forgo his own desires and needs for the sake of his beloved friend. How much greater is a marriage relationship when Christ is at the center of it (the third braid in the bonding cord). Since God never gives up on us, you should never give up on your spouse.

TAKE ACTION

- Make a written declaration to your spouse what you are willing to commit to in your marriage. Be specific in stating several things in what you are intentionally committing to, such as,"I commit to provide support and encouragement to you when you are suffering through difficulties." Date your commitment statements and give them to each other.

PRAY

Him: • Ask God to give you the qualities of a true, loyal friend to your wife, even through the hardest times.

Her: • Ask God to give you a lasting loyalty towards your husband, especially when he doesn't deserve it.

BEING LOYAL, Part 2

[3]Never let loyalty and kindness leave you! Tie them around your neck as a reminder. Write them deep within your heart. [4]Then you will find favor with both God and people, and you will earn a good reputation.
— Proverbs 3:3–4

Although this is good advice for life in general, it is excellent advice when applied to the marriage relationship. Your marriage is a sacred covenant made with God and your spouse. But it is also a spiritual discipline designed to help you know God better, trust Him wholeheartedly, and love Him more deeply.

The ESV translation of this verse states that you shouldn't let "steadfast love" and "faithfulness" abandon you. That is covenant language. As a husband shows love and faithfulness to his wife, so a wife should show love and faithfulness to her husband. This is the analogy of a covenantal marriage — God is the husband and His people are the wife/bride. Marriage is meant to make you holy.

> "Everything about your marriage — everything — is filled with prophetic potential, with the capacity for discovering and revealing Christ's character.
> • The respect you accord your partner;
> • the forgiveness you humbly seek and graciously extend;
> • the ecstasy, awe, and sheer fun of lovemaking;
> • the history you and your spouse build with one another.
> These and other facets of your marriage uncover the mystery of God's overarching purpose.
>
> "Because whether it is delightful or difficult, your marriage can become a doorway to a closer walk with God, and to a spiritual integrity that, like salt, seasons the world around you and with the savor of Christ.
>
> "The most fulfilling message about marriage: together, you have the capacity for sacredness, for a God-honoring, other-empowering, self-sacrificing purpose that brings joy now and impact forever."*

**Sacred Marriage.* Copyright © 2000 and 2015 by Gary L. Thomas, Zondervan, Grand Rapids, MI

Give honor to marriage and remain faithful to one another in marriage.
— Hebrews 13:4

When you marry, loyalty and kindness are to be embedded within you. It's the very nature of Jesus that we show to our spouse. To tie these attributes around your neck and write them on your heart means to never forget them and that they should show in all our mannerisms.

This shows blessings follow obedience (see page 184). Notice in verse 3 the items we are to obey. Then blessings follow: favor with God and people, earning you a good reputation. If you obediently covenant with God, you'll achieve success. God is teaching you, for your good, how He set things up in the world to function. He will always commit to His covenant with us.

He always stands by his covenant — the commitment he made to a thousand generations.
— Psalm 105:8

The maximum marriage commits to the covenant made with God. *This* is what brings joy and peace to the relationship with your spouse, with God, and with other people.

TAKE ACTION

- Tell your spouse out loud, "During good times and bad, I'm all in. It may not be a walk in the park, but it's worth it. I'm dedicated to serving you. I'm dedicated to making our marriage work always."

PRAY

Him: • As you pray out loud with your wife, commit to God that you will always be filled with a loyal love to your wife.

Her: • As you pray out loud with your husband, commit to God that you will always fight for the good of your marriage.

BEING LOYAL, Part 3

Loyalty makes a person attractive.

— Proverbs 19:22a

This Proverb has been translated many different ways. For our study, let's concentrate on the first part alone. Observe the variations:

- NIV: What a person desires is unfailing love...."
- AMP: "That which is desirable in a man is his loyalty and unfailing love."
- ESV: "What is desired in a man is steadfast love...."
- NKJV: "What is desired in a man is kindness...."
- CSB: "What is desirable in a person is his fidelity...."
- LBT: "Kindness makes a man attractive."

Unfailing love, steadfast love, kindness, and fidelity are just some of the variations translated into our language. But I like the NLT because it wraps all those up in loyalty. If you have any, or all these traits, you are attractive to others. A loyal person is one who is faithful, steadfast, loving, and kind. We all desire to have others like us and here is the key: be loyal.

He who earnestly seeks righteousness and loyalty finds life, righteousness, and honor.

— Proverbs 21:21 (AMP)

Loyalty isn't something you can just say you have. It is an undertaking you carry out over time with your actions. Here are 5 qualities of a loyal relationship:

1. A loyal relationship is supportive. A loyal person cares enough to stay aware, and take action when they know you need a pick-me-up, or just a little reminder to stay on track. (Rom. 12:10)

2. A loyal relationship is respectful. A loyal person will be respectful of you and will decline the opportunity to spread gossip. (1 Peter 2:17; Prov. 25:9–10)

3. A loyal relationship is trustworthy. A loyal person loves you (and only you) fully and completely. (1 Cor. 13:7)

4. A loyal relationship is sincere. A loyal person is faithful in a way that shows up during the good times and the bad times. Loyal people are supportive (even loving) for no other reason than they care. They practice random acts of kindness continually. (Prov. 27:10)

5. A loyal relationship has integrity. The loyal person properly cares for themselves and others around them. When they make a mistake, they will readily apologize. It's important to them to uphold good character and moral righteousness.* (Titus 2:7)

The game is my wife. It demands loyalty and responsibility, and it gives me back fulfillment and peace.
— Michael Jordan

Loyalty is displayed through love, devotion, dedication, and commitment to the well being of another. That's attractive!

The foundation stones for a balanced success are honesty, character, integrity, faith, love and loyalty.
— Zig Ziglar

TAKE ACTION

- Look up the verses associated with the 5 qualities of a loyal relationship and hand write them on note paper to help you remember them.

PRAY

Him: • Pray Romans 12:10 this way: "I will love [*wife's name*] with genuine affection, and take delight in honoring her all the time."

Her: • Pray 1 Corinthians 13:7 this way: "My love for [*husband's name*] will never give up, never lose faith, will always be hopeful, and will endure through every circumstance."

* Taken from powerofpositivity.com

CHOOSING CHRIST-CENTERED ACTIONS

Commit your actions to the LORD, and your plans will succeed.
— Proverbs 16:3

Our Lord committed a phenomenal action to show His love for us by dying on the cross. In the same manner, a husband and wife should daily commit to show the same phenomenal love towards each other.

When you agreed to get married, you committed to an action of becoming husband and wife. For richer or poorer. Through sickness and health. To love and cherish till death. If you vow to do something, you mean you're committing to that action.

A successful marriage requires setting plans or goals to accomplish together — *in agreement* — throughout the journey of married life. Plans like where you're going to live, what church you'll attend, and how many children you'll have, etc. To succeed, however, the vision you share as a team should always bring God glory.

Where there is no vision, the people perish: but he that keepeth the law, happy is he.
— Proverbs 29:18 (KJV)

Committing your works and plans to God means surrendering them to God's will (see James 4:13–15), trusting that God will be glorified in them, and recognizing that it is not in your power to properly guide your own steps. Like when Jesus demonstrated His love for us, when you commit your plans and works to the Lord, you are saying, "Not my will, Father, but yours be done!"

Let the word of Christ dwell in you richly in all wisdom, teaching and admonishing one another in psalms and hymns and spiritual songs, singing with grace in your hearts to the Lord. And whatever you do in word or deed, do all in the name of the Lord Jesus, giving thanks to God the Father through Him.

— Colossians 3:16–17 (NKJV)

Interestingly, Proverbs 16:9 says, "We can make our plans, but the LORD determines our steps." At first glance, you might think this verse contradicts today's verse. On the contrary, they relate to each other. While you may make plans for the future and propose a course of action, ultimately God is in control. (See Proverbs 20:24). The key is to be in God's will.

Take all your actions and commit them to the Lord. God will make your plans succeed. Your plans may not always go the way you thought they would. A change of course could mean that God is just redirecting you to line up with His will. How things eventually work out is just an amazing thing to witness. Trust God and be in tune with Him (See pages 20 and 30). Rely on Him for success in your life and in your marriage.

Commit everything you do to the Lord. Trust Him, and He will help you.

— Psalm 37:5

TAKE ACTION

- Have a vision meeting and discuss goals and plans of what you'd like to accomplish in the coming year. Discuss if these plans will glorify God.

PRAY

Him:
- Commit your marriage and every action you do within it to God.
- Ask for God's blessings on your plans.

Her:
- Praise God for being in control of your marriage and plans.

DISCIPLINING FOR LIFE

People who accept discipline are on the pathway to life, but those who ignore correction will go astray.

— Proverbs 10:17

By now, you've discovered (or will someday discover) marriage takes discipline. Some say it's hard work. I like to say it just takes effort. And it's not really that hard if you commit to putting in the effort.

When you consider making a committed effort at anything in life, you believe a reward will result. The more effort you put in, the more reward you will reap. It's the same when investing in your marriage.

Solomon explains the pathway to life requires disciplined effort. I don't know about you, but I would much rather be on a pathway to life over a pathway to death. Do you want to get in shape? You will have to work out. The more effort you put into your regimen, the better the results.

Yes, it's hard, no doubt about it. Look at how the writer of Hebrews tells it like it is:

No discipline is enjoyable while it is happening — it's painful! But afterward there will be a peaceful harvest of right living for those who are trained in this way.

— Hebrews 12:11

Dave Willis says, "Great marriages don't happen by luck or by accident. They are the result of a consistent investment of:

- time
- thoughtfulness
- forgiveness
- affection
- prayer
- mutual respect
- and a rock-solid commitment between both husband and wife."

These attributes will require a little effort and a continual management (commitment). The results will be worth it.

If you have children, you know you must discipline them. This is part of growing up and learning. You probably don't like to discipline them, but know it's for their own good. Undisciplined children get into more trouble and are harder to manage.

My child, don't reject the LORD's discipline, and don't be upset when he corrects you. For the LORD corrects those he loves, just as a father corrects a child in whom he delights.

— Proverbs 3:11–12

To learn, you must love discipline; it is stupid to hate correction.

— Proverbs 12:1

Joyful are those you discipline, LORD, those you teach with your instructions.

— Psalm 94:12

Commitment in marriage involves obedience to God. Obedience requires discipline. Accept discipline and correction. Reap rewards.

TAKE ACTION

- Study Hebrews 12:5–11 on how discipline relates to God's love.

PRAY

Him:
- Ask God to give you a willingness to be disciplined.
- Thank God for giving you the pathway to a great life through His discipline.

Her:
- Ask God to give you a more disciplined effort towards each of the areas quoted on page 114 by Dave Willis.

☐☐ MAKING THE EFFORT TO IMPROVE

All hard work brings a profit, but mere talk leads only to poverty.
— Proverbs 14:23 (NIV)

I tend to cringe when someone says "marriage is hard work." If it was, why would anyone want to get married in the first place? It is not a ball and chain lifestyle. It is not slaving away in a rock quarry.

Learning to live with someone day in and day out for the rest of your life takes effort. Observe this way of thinking from Fawn Weaver, founder of Happy Wives Club:

> "Change the thought that marriage is "hard work." Most of us are underpaid and underappreciated for the work we do. When you call marriage "work," you subconsciously tell yourself you are giving more than you are receiving. But when you use words like "effort" or "investment," there is an expectation there will be a reward. The more effort you put in the more reward you will get out. The more investment you put in, the larger the dividend that pays out. By changing the phrase,"marriage is hard work," to "marriage takes effort," you have just changed how you see marriage."

Marriage is meant to be an amazing adventure with the love of your life. Surely it's worth a little "effort" and "investment." And it's really not that hard when you make the concentrated effort to have a strong marriage.

Marriage has the power to set the course of your life as a whole. If your marriage is strong, even if all the circumstances in your life around you are filled with trouble and weakness, it won't matter. You will be able to move out into the world in strength.
— Timothy Keller, *The Meaning of Marriage*

---

*From the blog of Fawn Weaver, Happy Wives Club, "Girlfriends' Guide to a Great Marriage: 3 Easy Ways You Can Strengthen Marriages Around You Every Day" posted February 12, 2014. happywivesclub.com

So when Solomon says hard work brings a profit, he is talking about a concentrated effort towards something. Making that effort in your relationship will bring these benefits: peace, joy, intimacy, satisfaction, and happiness, among others.

Love is an action verb. You can say, "I love you," but your actions will demonstrate it in actuality. As Solomon says that mere talk leads to poverty, it means if you don't actively make the effort to show your love for your spouse, the relationship will become impoverished.

A good marriage doesn't happen by itself. It must be maintained. What you put into it is what you'll get out of it. You don't plant a garden and then expect it you give you a harvest without any cultivating.

A good marriage isn't something you find; it's something you make, and you have to keep on making it.

— Gary L. Thomas

A maximum marriage commits to the effort of continual maintenance. Small daily actions are not that hard, but add up to big dividends over the long run.

TAKE ACTION

- Read Gary Thomas' book, *A Lifelong Love: How to Have Lasting Intimacy, Friendship, and Purpose in Your Marriage.*

PRAY

Him:

- Ask God to give you the drive to continually invest in your marriage.
- Thank God for the journey and adventure in your marriage.

Her:

- Ask God to keep you from seeing your relationship as work, but as a journey of growth and harvest.

PLANTING A BOUNTIFUL GARDEN

[30]I walked by the field of a lazy person, the vineyard of one with no common sense. [31]I saw that it was overgrown with nettles. It was covered with weeds and its walls were broken down. [32]Then, as I looked and thought about it, I learned this lesson: [33]A little extra sleep, a little more slumber, a little folding of the hands to rest — [34]then poverty will pounce on you like a bandit; scarcity will attack you like an armed robber.

— Proverbs 24:30–34 (See also Proverbs 6:10–11)

What a sad picture this is of an overgrown vineyard. This person had obviously acquired some nice land, but failed to maintain it. Solomon jabs lazy people throughout Proverbs. They are sarcastically compared to a door that swings back and forth (Prov. 26:14), and ridiculed for their empty excuses (Prov. 22:13). Solomon equates lazy people as fools, with their lack of productivity leading to poverty and death.

Despite their desires, the lazy will come to ruin, for their hands refuse to work.

— Proverbs 21:25

In contrast, diligent people are seen as wise. Their activities lead to wealth and life.

...Hard workers get rich. ...Those who work hard will prosper.

— Proverbs 10:4b; 13:4b

Marriage is much like a vineyard or garden. When you plant your relationship at the wedding ceremony, the work is only beginning. If you think your love will always sustain your marriage, it won't. It's the opposite — your marriage, being continually worked on, is what will sustain your love.

Marriage follows the law of the harvest, which states that only patient, wise effort over time will result in a good crop. Are great gardens just happy accidents? Not at all, and neither are great marriages. One should never assume the marriage will automatically grow on it's own. Just as you dated each other before you married, you must continue to pursue and date each other afterward.

A garden requires patient labor and attention. Plants do not grow merely to satisfy ambitions or to fulfill good intentions. They thrive because someone expended effort on them.
— Liberty Hyde Bailey, horticulturist and botanist

Weeds that grow in a garden are due to laziness. Weeds that spring up in a marriage are due to selfishness and pride. In contrast, the nutrients of grace, when received and acted upon by working faith, keep your garden green and healthy. You'll never think the grass is greener on the other side when your focus is on your own grass. A maximum marriage has two master gardeners making the effort to produce good fruit, being diligent and intentional.

TAKE ACTION

- Plan a weekend date, just the two of you.
- If you don't have one, discuss planting a garden, with the intent of gardening it together.
- Let today's Proverb be a reminder to always work on your marriage.

PRAY

Him: • Ask God to keep you focused on the effort required to have a bountiful marriage.

Her: • Ask God to make your garden flourish by your patient labor and attention.

☐☐ LOOKING FOR GOOD, Part 1

If you search for good, you will find favor; but if you search for evil, it will find you!
— Proverbs 11:27

If you have been married for any length of time, you have come to realize your partner will mess up. A maximum marriage relationship learns to look past the flaws. It takes patience. Concentrating on the good characteristics of the other person brings about more marital satisfaction.

If you look for the bad, you'll find it. However, if you're looking for goodwill from your spouse and focusing on their complimentary qualities, you may even be surprised by the number you find. Solomon says you'll find favor. Favor is approval, support, or a liking for someone. It makes sense that by finding favor, you'll grow deeper in love.

Seeing the good qualities in another takes a keen focus. But this proverb is also directed to personally doing good towards others. The ESV translation says whoever diligently seeks good gives us the interpretation to do good to others.

So in everything, do to others what you would have them do to you.
— Matthew 7:12 (NIV)

If you focus on the things of God you will become godly. If you focus on the things of the world you will become worldly. Your focus and expectation is the key. If you have it in your heart to be a blessing to others, you will always find opportunities through which you can be a blessing.

Your mother probably once told you on your way out of the house, "Stay out of trouble." The person who seeks mischief, who is always on the lookout for ways to do wrong, will find all sorts of opportunities to get into trouble. As the saying goes, "What goes around comes around." Our moms should have told us when we headed out, "Look for good!"

The highway of the upright avoids evil; those who guard their ways preserve their lives.

— Proverbs 16:17 (NIV)

Do you realize how this pertains to any circumstance? If you go into a situation dreading it or thinking how it will go wrong, it will. For instance, when you go to church looking for the good that God is doing, you'll see it. When you concentrate on what bothers you about the worship service, that's all you'll see. And you'll miss out on what God is doing. If you don't see good in circumstances right away, be patient. Your focus on the good will eventually reveal it.

Look for the good in your spouse. Concentrate on doing good towards your spouse. The message is simple, clear, and yet profound — you will basically find what you are searching for. Searching for and doing good will allow you to obtain favor and it'll glorify God.

TAKE ACTION

- Do something good today to make your spouse's day easier.
- Acknowledge each other's good qualities.

PRAY

Him:
- Tell God His good qualities and thank Him for them.
- Ask God to show you favor as you seek goodness in all of your life.

Her:
- Ask God to give you continual and patient focus on the good of others.
- Tell God that you'll commit to do good to glorify Him daily.

☐☐ LOOKING FOR GOOD, Part 2

Fools show their annoyance at once, but the prudent overlook an insult.
— Proverbs 12:16 (NIV)

Little insults are bound to come up in husband-wife conversations from time to time. Some may be intentional, some may slip out without realizing it. I've been known to say things that come out all wrong, and before I know it, Connie is offended and upset.

God has gifted her, however, with a gracious amount of patience. When those times of inappropriate words fall from my mouth, she has learned to not make a big deal about it — if the wound is small enough. She knows I'm not perfect. If I have wounded her greater than I realize, she will let me know that the remark hurt. Otherwise, she portrays the prudent person in this proverb and moves on.

Do you realize how this avoids so many hassles and conflicts? Research has proved this proverb. Blaine Flowers at the University of Miami has studied what he calls "marital illusions." These are the fantasies and unrealistic ideas people hold in marriage in general and their partners in particular. He's found that happy couples idealize their spouses, attributing more positive qualities to them than to anyone else. They also give their spouses credit for more positive aspects of the marriage than themselves.[1]

In short, the higher a couple's capacity to overlook potentially harmful remarks, the more marital satisfaction they enjoy. A prudent person is one who is wise, caring, and has thoughtful insight towards the future.

Fools vent their anger, but the wise quietly hold it back.
— Proverbs 29:11

Sensible people control their temper; they earn respect by overlooking wrongs.
— Proverbs 19:11

True love is loving the unlovable. When your spouse is revealing his or her worst is when you need to show love the most. What a revealing portrait of how our patient God loves you!

Oh, what joy for those whose disobedience is forgiven, whose sin is put out of sight! Yes, what joy for those whose record the LORD *has cleared of guilt, whose lives are lived in complete honesty!*

— Psalm 32:1–2

The gospel song proclaims God's love for us, "He saw the best in me, when everyone else around me, could only see the worst in me. He's mine and I'm His, it doesn't matter what I did. He only sees me for who I am."[2] What a beautiful way to express your love in the same way towards your spouse.

The maximum marriage is one that continually sees the good in each other, overlooking the annoyances. Patience is a beautiful characteristic to portray. Building patience will increase marital happiness.

▪ TAKE ACTION

- Weigh the benefits of overlooking something that hurt your feelings. It can be worth the extra effort of patience to avoid stirring up unneeded conflict.
- Tell each other the good qualities you see in each other.

▪ PRAY

Him:
- Ask God for you to be prudent in overlooking your wife's annoyances.
- Thank God for His patient love towards you.

Her:
- Ask God for prudence, patience and an ever-growing eye towards the good qualities in your husband.
- Thank God for His patient love towards you.

---

1. *Proverbs for Couples*, Les & Leslie Parrot, ©1997, Zondervan Publishing
2. "The Best In Me" written By Marvin Sapp & Aaron W. Lindsey, 2010

PERSEVERING OVER CONTROLLING

Better to be patient than powerful; better to have self-control than to conquer a city.

— Proverbs 16:32

Patience and self-control go hand in hand as virtues that need constant cultivating. Another translation of this Proverb says, "whoever is slow to anger is better than the mighty" (ESV). Being even-tempered takes self-control, and along with some patience added in.

Do you get impatient throughout a typical day? Unfortunately, you can get most impatient with the people closest to you, such as your spouse. It can be human-nature to try to control others and circumstances around us to conform to our preferred pace of life.

Here, Solomon says self-control is superior to trying to control someone else's behavior. Success in business, school, or home life can be ruined by a person who loses his or her temper. So it is a great personal victory to control your temper. When you feel yourself ready to explode, remember that losing control may cause you to forfeit what you want the most [*Life Application Study Bible* study note, page 1028].

Whoever is patient has great understanding, but one who is quick-tempered displays folly.

— Proverbs 14:29 (NIV)

Ultimately, you have to trust God and His timing. He has an eternal perspective you cannot see. Cultivating patience — especially with your spouse — will create an added benefit: peace.

Always be humble and gentle. Be patient with each other, making allowance for each other's faults because of your love. Make every effort to keep yourselves united in the Spirit, binding yourselves together with peace.

— Ephesians 4:2–3

Peace is another virtue given by the Holy Spirit. If you are upset and disturbed, you're not really trusting God that He can handle the situation. You are strongest when you hold your peace in every situation. Step back and give it over to God. If you allow your temper to flair up, you're opening the door for Satan to waltz in and destroy all semblance of order (See Ephesians 4:26–27).

Hot tempers cause arguments, but patience brings peace.
— Proverbs 15:18 (GNT)

And let the peace that comes from Christ rule in your hearts. For as members of one body you are called to live in peace. And always be thankful.
— Colossians 3:15

A maximum marriage models an attitude of patience. A patient husband and wife is a power couple. By controlling their own temperament, and not trying to control the other, a sense of peace will surround their home and relationship. They become conquerors by letting God take control.

TAKE ACTION

- Ask for forgiveness if you have been impatient with your spouse lately or trying to control him or her.
- Read Romans 8:37 in reference to today's Proverb.

PRAY

Him:
- Ask God to not allow your unbridled emotions to rule.
- Ask God for self-control and to grow your trust in Him.

Her:
- Ask God for perseverance and patience in all circumstances.
- Thank God for giving you His peace that can pass all human understanding.

AVOIDING THE DRIP

A quarrelsome wife is as annoying as constant dripping on a rainy day. Stopping her complaints is like trying to stop the wind or trying to hold something with greased hands.

— Proverbs 27:15–16 (See also Proverbs 19:13b)

Conflicts and arguments are inevitable in a marriage. The two of you are separate individuals created by God, each with your own strengths and weaknesses. Aiming for a secure, maximum marriage should always be the goal, and to grow closer through the disputes.

Rather than coming down hard on the wives here, I believe quarrels can go both ways. Husbands can be as quarrelsome as wives. And if you are the one doing the nagging, how has that worked out for you? Constant complaining never gets you anywhere. The description in this passage, if you take it to go both ways, says that unresolved fights between spouses is like a constant drip. It's annoying!

How do you stop a faucet from dripping or a roof that leaks? Maintenance. Your relationship must always be in constant repair deliberately by *both* of you. The longer the dripping continues by one or the other, the weaker you'll be when the storms come.

Starting a quarrel is like opening a floodgate, so stop before a dispute breaks out.

— Proverbs 17:14

Avoiding a fight is a mark of honor; only fools insist on quarreling.

— Proverbs 20:3

So how do you stop the quarrels if they're inevitable? Love, gentleness, and kindness. If your voice is raised, it will soon become a shouting match between the two of you. And you'll get nowhere. Name calling or lame excuses are likened to children fighting. Proverbs 15:1 says gentle words turn away wrath. Yelling doesn't solve anything. A good way to begin resolving a conflict is to say, "I agree." In spite of your differences, there may be areas that you can agree on. Look to build on those.

Solomon also explains it is better to live in an attic or in a desert than to share a house with a quarrelsome wife (Prov. 21:9; 21:19). This doesn't mean to get out and file for divorce. Avoidance of a conflict will not make it disappear. Seek to edify and unify, calmly and lovingly.

James 1:4 states, "What is causing the quarrels and fights among you? Don't they come from the evil desires at war within you?" Being a quarrelsome person stems from your own inner pride. *He* or *she* is not the problem. So many times we point the finger at others when really the problem is within us.

Stopping complaints is likened to trying to stop the wind. Today's Proverb seems to say it's impossible in verse 16. But it is in keeping with verse 15 describing the constant dripping. A constant drip can be fixed with maintenance. It won't be easy — you might have to twist the wrench extremely tight — but it can be done. Make a point to try it with grace.

TAKE ACTION

- Set a ground rule for resolving a conflict by declaring no yelling.
- Pray together before attempting to resolve an issue.

PRAY

Him:
- Ask God to keep you calm during the storms.
- Seek wisdom from God in how you can establish harmony.

Her:
- Ask God for contentment, and not to focus on your husband's faults.
- Ask God on how you can extend grace, rather than complaints.

CHILL

Whoever restrains his words has knowledge, and he who has a cool spirit is a man of understanding.

— Proverbs 17:27 (ESV)

Keeping a cool head can be difficult when your spouse is pushing the wrong buttons. Anger management is essential for a maximum marriage. We are ordered to forgive each other as we are forgiven in Christ without limit, reservation, or restriction (Ephesians 4:32). Paul also says in Ephesians 4:26 that anger gives a foothold to the devil. Make an effort to keep Christ at the center of your marriage at *all* times.

1 Peter 4:8 says, "Show deep love for each other, for love covers a multitude of sins." Observe how love is the opposite of anger:

- Love is kind; anger is mean.
- Love does not boast; anger makes others feel small.
- Love is selfless; anger is selfish.
- Love soothes; anger increases pain.
- Love sees into eternity; anger can't see past its own nose.*

A hot-tempered man stirs up dissension, but a patient man calms a quarrel.

— Proverbs 15:18

Take note of these simple anger management tips:

1. **Think before you spout off** — Take a few moments to collect your thoughts before saying anything (or count to 10) — and allow your spouse to do so also.
2. **In a calm way, express your anger** — As soon as you're calm, express your frustration in an assertive but nonconfrontational way. Don't try to hurt your spouse or control them.
3. **Take a timeout** — Mutually agree to have a timeout of an agreed amount of time if things are not getting resolved.

**Fierce Marriage*, Copyright © 2018 by Ryan and Selena Frederick; Baker Book Publishing Group

4. **Look for possible solutions** — If you focus on the facts of where you disagree, finding a solution will be easier.
5. **Use 'I' statements** — Avoid criticizing or placing blame. Use "I" statements to describe how you are feeling. Be respectful and specific. For example, say, "I'm upset that you didn't offer to help with the dishes" instead of "You never do any housework."
6. **Seek help** — Don't be ashamed to ask a Christian counselor for help if your anger seems out of control.

He who is slow to anger is better than the mighty, And he who rules his spirit, than he who captures a city.
— Proverbs 16:32 (NASB)

Now you might think that suppressing anger would be a good way to keep the peace in the house. This is not so. Suppressors will tend to get depressed and eventually explode resulting in further conflicts. It's alright to go to bed with an unresolved conflict, as long as both of you agree to a truce and to work on a resolution the next day. Control the drama and focus on resolutions politely, and in a courteous manner. Spread grace. Choose to love in a kind way.

TAKE ACTION

- Talk about laying some ground rules on how you should discuss disagreements before a squabble breaks out.
- Talk about what gets under your skin or your buttons that get pushed in the wrong way.

PRAY

Him:
- Ask God to help you chill.
- Thank God for peaceful resolutions.

Her:
- Ask God for forgiveness if you are typically the one who spouts off.
- Ask God to fill you with His love and to portray that love at all times.

KEEPING THE PEACE, Part 1

A gentle answer deflects anger, but harsh words make tempers flare.
— Proverbs 15:1

Would it be possible to argue in a whisper? It's also hard to argue with someone who keeps answering back in a quiet, calm way. If you raise your voice and use harsh words, you'll most likely encounter angry words reflected back on you. Peacefulness isn't found in loud, rude, discourteous, or abusive words.

The husband and wife who can stay controlled and calm during what might be considered a heated discussion, will resolve the issue quicker. Surely, you desire a peaceful environment in your relationship.

Patience can persuade a prince, and soft speech can break bones.
— Proverbs 25:15

Consider the following list of derogatory encounters and determine the ones you use and the ones your spouse uses, then discuss them. But not during a dispute, only at a peaceful time. You can even rank them by the ones you feel you each resort to the most.

- Bad Timing. Pick the worst time to start an argument.
- Escalating. Move quickly from a single issue to more significant matters you've been waiting to bring up.
- Sand Bagging. Move from the primary issue to all the other problems you have.
- Generalizing. Use inflammatory language like "always" and "never."
- Cross-Complaining. Respond to their complaints with one of your own.
- Interrogating. Imply with a question that they could have easily done something that they didn't. For example, "Why didn't you..."
- Blaming. Make the issue entirely their fault.
- Pulling Rank. Make the point that you do more than them in every area.
- Dominating. Talk over them regardless of what they say.
- Violation Listing. Recite every injustice you've suffered.
- Negative Labeling. Give the person a negative psychological label like "immature" or "neurotic."
- Mind Reading. Telling the person why they did something even if you don't know.

- Predicting. Predict fatalistic views of the future.
- Avoiding Ownership. Don't take responsibility for anything.
- Exiting. Walk out of the room or leave the house in protest.
- Denying Compromise. Never back down from your position.
- Personalizing. Make it about the person and not the issue.
- Victimizing. Make yourself the eternal martyr.
- Grudging. Hold a grudge forever and bring it up over and over again.
- Shifting. Be inconsistent in an argument to avert resolution.

Marriage is not about winning and losing; it's about oneness. When one person loses, you both lose, and when one person wins, you both win. Oneness is about a husband and wife becoming so intimately connected that you develop a mental, physical, relational, and spiritual harmony. But occasionally in an effort to find oneness you'll have conflict. It's common to have disagreements, conflicts, arguments, or fights. Call them what you want, but seek common understanding.* Peacefully. With gentle answers. (See also Expressing Gentleness, pages 62–65)

You can't win an argument. You can't because if you lose it, you lose it; and if you win it, you lose it.
— Dale Carnegie

Do all that you can to live in peace with everyone.
— Romans 12:18

TAKE ACTION

- Patiently, peacefully and calmly, talk about the list above of harsh encounters. Don't criticize but talk about seeking oneness.

PRAY

Him: • Ask God to help you employ peace and oneness within your house and in your relationship.

Her: • Thank God for a peaceful household.

*sermoncentral.com, Dirty Fighting Techniques In Marriage Series, contributed by Vince Miller.

KEEPING THE PEACE, Part 2

Without wood a fire goes out; without a gossip a quarrel dies down. As charcoal to embers and as wood to fire, so is a quarrelsome person for kindling strife.

— Proverbs 26:20–21 (NIV)

One of the most successful, longest-running advertising icons was created by the U.S. Forest Service called Smokey the Bear. His slogan, "Only You Can Prevent Forest Fires," was created in 1947 and later updated in 2001 to "Only You Can Prevent Wildfires."

That's what Solomon says about quarreling. We can turn down the heat, douse the fire, and let the argument die. You can prevent the fire by *not* supplying juicy morsels of gossip (or charcoal). Without a fire-starter, an ugly dispute can dissolve and relationships can heal.

Some people love to quarrel and disagree and debate. They stir up fights with hurtful words and keep the fights flaming higher and higher. They are essentially childish "tattletales." They're hard to get along with. Not many people want to be around them. In Proverbs 13:10, Solomon nails the issue, which is pride as the reason that leads to conflict. These prideful people add wood to fires to make them hotter and larger, similar to an out-of-control wildfire.

Solomon goes on to say in Proverbs 15:18, "A hot-tempered person starts fights; a cool-tempered person stops them." So the fire preventer is cool, gracious, and a peacemaker. God calls you to be a peacemaker (Rom. 12:18) and that you'll be blessed (Matt. 5:9). Peace is a fruit of the Spirit. A peacemaker is one who excels in dishing out mercy.

A person's wisdom yields patience; it is to one's glory to overlook an offense.

— Proverbs 19:11 (NIV) (See also Proverbs 20:3)

Whoever would love life and see good days must keep their tongue from evil and their lips from deceitful speech. They must turn from evil and do good; they must seek peace and pursue it.

— 1 Peter 3:10–11 (NIV)

Work at living in peace with everyone, and work at living a holy life....

— Hebrews 12:14

Living in peaceful harmony with another person day in and day out requires a deliberate daily practice of pursuing peace. When you walk in married peace, you don't demand your rights, you seek the best interest of your spouse. Instead of returning an insult for an insult, you return a blessing. When disappointed, you don't become passive aggressive to make sure your spouse knows how dissatisfied you are. When angered, you don't focus on the person's failure, and you'll do your best not to make the problem worse.

A kindled fire never goes out. Make sure what you're kindling in your marriage is peace filled with love.

▩ TAKE ACTION

- Resolve to prevent conflicts from flaring up with hurtful words. Be calm, cool, and gracious peacemakers.

▩ PRAY

Him:
- Ask God to make you a fire preventer and not a starter.
- Ask God for you to keep kindling the fire of love.

Her:
- Ask God for forgiveness if you have entertained hurtful words towards your spouse. Ask Him to help you heal the hurt.
- Thank God for peace.

☐☐ KEEPING THE PEACE, Part 3

Starting a quarrel is like opening a floodgate, so stop before a dispute breaks out.

— Proverbs 17:14

There are those who love drama and chaos and will create it just so their life is interesting. Their lives have become mundane, boring, and predictable. The drama sparks excitement. "Drama kings" and "drama queens" fail to realize they can change their behavior and lives for the better by discovering their passion or purpose for living.

Quarrelling is one way they create drama and chaos. But it is the wrong way to a peaceful life. Solomon says creating drama, such as an argument, opens the floodgates. Have you ever seen water gushing outward from a dam when the gates are opened up? It's a powerful force! Preventive maintenance has been our theme for resolving conflicts.

I have come to the conclusion that there is only one way under high heaven to get the best of an argument — and that is to avoid it. Avoid it as you would avoid rattlesnakes and earthquakes.

— Dale Carnegie

Any fool can start arguments; the honorable thing is to stay out of them.

— Proverbs 20:3 (GNT)

If you're living with a drama king or queen, how do you avoid the chaos they create and make a peaceful resolution? Here are three ways:

1. Stay off their stage. They would like nothing better than to include you in their performance. Stay apart and don't get sucked in. Keep your peace intact.

2. Remember it's not your show. Whatever reasoning they have to create this drama, realize it doesn't have to be your story. You can calmly tell them, "When you start this type of arguing, it makes me feel hurt. I would feel better if you calmed down and we could talk quietly."

3. Bring down the curtain with boundaries. Boundaries keep you safe. Know what you will tolerate, and what you won't. Do what's in your best interest and theirs. If you can't listen, say so. If you need to create some space, create it. Tell them what you will and won't tolerate. And then know what you will do if it's crossed. And stick to it. You may not always have a choice about which experiences may become a crisis drama, but you can choose how you respond.

Better a dry crust eaten in peace than a house filled with feasting—and conflict.

— Proverbs 17:1

Look hard at yourself and see if you're a dramatist. I'll say it so your spouse doesn't have to, "Lose it." Try to understand why you may be creating this diversion or stimulus. Look for what your passion in life is. You have a God-given gift. Ask your spouse what they think you're really good at, what adds value to your life and to others. Then pursue that. It will create a peaceful relationship, one that you subconsciously really desire.

TAKE ACTION

- Whenever you see conflict brewing, step back and put on the brakes before the floodgates open. Be peaceful and calm.
- You can have disagreements. Agree to disagree on certain things. Quarrelling won't get you anywhere.

PRAY

Him: • Ask God to give you a sense of peace and self-control in stopping disputes before they break out.

Her: • Ask God for a maximum marriage filled with peace.

GETTING PAST THE HURT

Sensible people control their temper; they earn respect by overlooking wrongs.

— Proverbs 19:11

If you've been injured by your spouse, it's human nature to want to retaliate. You're hurt, you're mad, and you want to make them feel the way they made you feel. Solomon is saying to us to be sensible; be patient and control your angry feelings. See Proverbs 20:22.

The nucleus of the gospel is centered around forgiveness. You cannot come to God without Christ's blood of forgiveness covering your sins. If every time you sinned, God got angry at you and was unforgiving, you would have no hope. Remember, He loves you in spite of your wrongdoings. You can face each new day knowing His mercies are new every morning (Lamentations 3:22–23). Praise God for that! So in likewise manner, you are to forgive your spouse of their offenses.

Make allowance for each other's faults, and forgive anyone who offends you. Remember, the Lord forgave you, so you must forgive others.

— Colossians 3:13

Therefore, accept each other just as Christ has accepted you so that God will be given glory.

— Romans 15:7

This doesn't mean you should just turn and look the other way when your spouse hurts you. Forgiveness doesn't excuse the other person's behavior, forgiveness prevents their behavior from destroying you. If you think that you just can't forgive someone because the hurt they caused is too severe, then you are allowing bitterness and resentment to grow within you. Those two traits will destroy your happiness. Let God handle the justice and allow Him to work on the offender.

Solomon declares the controlled forgiver earns respect. It is a virtue. Forgiveness is embedded within each of the nine fruit of the Spirit (Galatians 5:22–23): love, peace, patience, kindness, goodness, faithfulness, gentleness, and self-control. See how the entirety of today's Proverb describes each of these virtues?

...Love covers all wrongs.

— Proverbs 10:12b (See also 1 Peter 4:8)

The hurt caused by your spouse is lessened when you turn it over to God. You are acting out the love of God by choosing forgiveness, and then the healing can begin. God paid a high price in offering His Son to die for your sins. Remember that high cost and remember His continual forgiveness to you. Struggling marriages can be revived by forgiveness; a maximum marriage is sustained by it.

TAKE ACTION

- Together, read Galatians 5:22–23 and talk about how forgiveness is required to exercise each of these virtues.
- Read 1 Corinthians 13:5 and discuss how it relates to today's Proverb.

PRAY

Him:
- Ask God to fill you with controlled forgiveness.
- Thank God that he has removed your sins as far as the east is from the west (Psalm 103:12).

Her:
- Ask God to give you calmness and patience when your husband does something that annoys or hurts you.
- Thank God for giving you righteousness through the blood of Jesus.

PROSPERING IN LOVE

Love prospers when a fault is forgiven, but dwelling on it separates close friends.

— Proverbs 17:9

Faults. Like it or not, we all have them. How marvelous that we have a Savior who forgives us in spite of our own failures! His love is our model in marriage.

This proverb can enrich your marriage. Because marriage is a familiar and intimate relationship with another, you will know more of your spouse's faults and failures than any other person. Can you cover, forgive, and overlook their shortcomings without continually badgering them? Do you think that bringing up their faults again and again helps either you or them?

Paul tells us in Ephesians 4:32 to be kind to each other, tenderhearted, forgiving one another, just as God through Christ has forgiven you. Cover your spouse with acts of kindness in spite of their imperfections. This is how the love of God grows and prospers between you.

Show deep love for each other, for love covers a multitude of sins.

— 1 Peter 4:8

Love keeps no record of wrongs.

— 1 Corinthians 13:5b (NIV)

This doesn't mean to ignore sins. If someone has done something grievously wrong to you, it needs to be mended. But it must be done in a gracious way. The following are four habits that can lead to forgiving faults and wrongs done to you by Christian blogger, Darlene Schacht (Time-Warp Wife):

1. Prayer – Acknowledge your pain and bring it to prayer. In many cases, your pain is justified. Forgiving doesn't mean that you weren't hurt, it just means that you won't let it define you. Ask God to take the burden away from you and to give you the wisdom and strength to forgive.

2. Humility – *Living* right will bring you so much further than *being* right ever will. Don't be afraid to walk in forgiveness and grace. Remind yourself that humility is a powerful choice to serve God and that forgiveness is one of the strongest steps you can take.

3. Wisdom – Forgiving someone doesn't mean that you excuse their behavior. In some cases you must put boundaries in place. Use wisdom in doing so. Search the scriptures, and if you're still unsure of how to handle your situation, seek wise Christian counseling from someone like your pastor.

4. Kindness – Don't use your words as ammunition. Don't say things that are unkind to them or about them. We must do what we can to soften our hearts and to love as Christ loved.*

Dwelling on offenses separates. Forgiveness unites. Forgiveness is the needle that mends. Choose to be gracious to your spouse in order to allow love to grow. After all, neither one of you are perfect. A maximum marriage is a forgiving marriage.

TAKE ACTION

- Make a point to give each other blessings today, such as, taking a walk together, leaving a love note somewhere, planning a date, giving a foot rub, giving a surprise kiss, etc. (See pages 156–157 for more ideas).
- Read Psalm 103:8–12 together.

PRAY

Him:
- Thank God for the saving blood of Jesus Christ.
- Ask God to fill you with prosperous love through forgiveness.

Her:
- Ask God to ease the pain of an offense and for Him to take the hurt from you.
- Thank God for His many blessings in your relationship.

CONNECTING THROUGH HONESTY

People who conceal their sins will not prosper, but if they confess and turn from them, they will receive mercy.
— Proverbs 28:13

When a husband and wife cannot connect intimately with one another, it is because one of them, or both of them, are walking in darkness in some area of their lives. If you walk in the light, as Jesus is in the light, you will have improved closeness with one another.

If we confess our sins to Him, he is faithful and just to forgive us our sins and to cleanse us from all wickedness.
— 1 John 1:9

You can only have fellowship with Christ by dealing with your sin. The way you do that is by confessing your sin and turning from it. Then, by the blood of Jesus you are cleansed from unrighteousness.

The Bible says we've all sinned and fallen short of the glory of God (Romans 3:23). However, God provided a way for all of us to be forgiven, and that way is through the blood of Jesus Christ on the cross.

The cross is our connection to God. Your sin breaks that connection. But God provides a re-connect through Jesus and the confession of your sin.

Perhaps you've tried to pull one over on God. You may have allowed something to enter your life you know is wrong and then try to give God the silent treatment. It's hard to be honest with Him or with others about your faults. So you try to hide it. You can even get very creative in making up stories that will cover your tracks, and keep you out of trouble.

You may get away with the sin for a while. But a person who conceals and hides his sin will never prosper. Why? Because a person who hides his or her sin is investing in a lie, and that lie will cause a person to grow farther from God, which will lead to emptiness.

In the same way, your relationship with your spouse requires full disclosure — no secrets. Hiding or attempted cover-up of your faults sets the relationship back — it breaks your connection. There can be no advancement without acknowledgment of a wrong. In other words, couples who conceal their wrongs will not prosper in marriage. But if they confess and refuse to return to those wrongs, they will receive mercy.

The last phrase in today's verse is imperative — "they *will* receive mercy." This means the one who was wronged must give mercy. It's a two-step process, one asks for forgiveness, the other forgives. Just as God forgives you.

Oh, what joy for those whose disobedience is forgiven, whose sin is put out of sight! Yes, what joy for those whose record the LORD *has cleared of guilt, whose lives are lived in complete honesty!*

— Psalm 32:1–2

TAKE ACTION

- Never bring up past wrongs that have been committed but are not being committed now. Look forward.
- Vow to each other to always be honest. It will always — *always* — help you grow and connect.

PRAY

Him:

- Thank God for wiping your slate clean and never remembering your past sins.
- Ask God to fill you with open honesty with Him and your wife.

Her:

- Thank Jesus for His mercy and grace in covering your sins.
- Ask God for complete honesty in your relationship with Him and your husband.

PURGING POWER

By mercy and truth iniquity is purged: and by the fear of the Lord men depart from evil.

— Proverbs 16:6 (KJV)

To purge means to completely remove or to wipe out entirely. And what purges our iniquity, or immoral behavior? The first is mercy.

Other translations use "unfailing love" or "steadfast love" for the word mercy. It's a strong love that never fails. It's a totally devoted love. Mercy is that loving compassion or forgiveness shown toward someone when it's within your power to punish or harm them.

The second purging power is truth. Other translations use "faithfulness." Truth is being loyal to what is right as revealed in the Word of God, and being sincere about pursing his Word.

A person who has put away their sin can only "purge" the guilty past by the practice of "mercy and truth." Forgiving yourself first is vital to being able to forgive others. Practice kindness, integrity, grace, and purity. Whenever you've done something that is wrong, false, or hurtful, now do that which is just, true, and right. Do that which is kind, helpful, and generous. Then you'll see that everything that was wrong is now purged to purity. Mercy and truth are two jewels of perfect godliness.

Mercy and truth are met together; Righteousness and peace have kissed each other.

— Psalm 85:10

Do mercy and truth kiss together in your life? Are you vigilant for the truth, *and* sensitive to the needs of others around you? Do you lead your children in the right way, *and* show them mercy and pity when they fail? Husband, do you lead your wife spiritually, *and* show honor to her? Wife, do you encourage your husband to pursue God, *and* still love him when he is not lovable?

Do you do the best in performing your job, *and* show mercy to the careless waitress who spills a drink in your lap? Do you always pay your bills on time, *and* show mercy to those who are late in paying you? Do you tell your associates the truth, *and* pray for them when they turn against you for it?

Mercy and truth are met together perfectly in our Lord Jesus Christ. Righteousness and peace have kissed each other in Him.

Then the question is how do we keep from falling again? The answer is by walking in reverence of the Spirit, by proceeding in "the fear of the Lord" (See more study on the fear of the Lord on page 10). This will result in abstracting yourself from the wrongs and thereby purposely pursuing good. When you cultivate a reverent spirit, realizing the presence of God, walking with God in prayer, and keeping your mind on the thoughts of God, you'll "be removed from your iniquity." You are redeemed! Now live the new and better life of faith and purity and love.

The husband and wife in a maximum marriage purge each other from wrongdoings by showing mercy and truth. Together, they fear the Lord and intentionally pursue the godly life. Their marriage shows righteousness and peace kissing each other.

TAKE ACTION

- Show the mercy of Jesus to each other on a daily basis.
- If either of you have slacked off in this study of Proverbs, give an encouraging word to get back on track.

PRAY

Him:

- Praise God for His mercy and truth!
- Praise God for peace within your home.

Her:

- Thank Jesus for His unfailing love!
- Ask God to show redemption to your husband in those moments when he annoys you.

GIVING FIRST FROM THE HEART

Honor the Lord *from your wealth, And from the first of all your produce; So your barns will be filled with plenty.*
— Proverbs 3:9–10 (NASB)

In order for you and your spouse to fully maximize all that God desires for your marriage, you must understand biblical principles of the resources He has provided to you. Solomon was an extremely wealthy man and he has much to say about money.

In the first place, managing the resources God has given to you should be done out of a grateful heart for His generous grace and provision. When someone does an act of kindness towards me, I want to repay them back with kindness. If you think about all the blessings God has given you and His kindness towards you, surely you would want to repay Him back in some way.

In his book, *Kingdom Marriage*, Tony Evans explains three simple words in the area of finance: **give, save, spend**. I believe this is great financial advice for anyone wanting to know the secret of obtaining wealth. I'll break down these three words through three separate devotionals. Today's Proverb is the first course of action, and that is to give.

Matthew 6:21 states that wherever your heart is, that is where your treasure is. Where is your heart? What are you passionate about? If I were to look at your bank account, what payment would I notice is debited first after your paycheck is deposited? The mortgage? The car payment? A credit card payment? Solomon says it plainly: Honor the Lord with the *first* payment that comes out of your paycheck.

Giving the first of what you're given is a tangible way of expressing your trust in God to meet all your needs. If you take the first for yourself and leave to God what is left over, you're implicating you're not confident the Lord can meet your needs. You're demonstrating a lack of faith if you take what you need first, and think you won't be satisfied. Most respected financial advisers (even those who don't believe God's Word) will tell their clients that giving has to be an integral part of their lives in order to be financially successful.

I've heard many couples say there's no way they can give a tithe to the church on what they make, and also pay all their bills. Read the following verse:

"Bring all the tithes into the storehouse so there will be enough food in my Temple. If you do," says the LORD *of Heaven's Armies, "I will open the windows of heaven for you. I will pour out a blessing so great you won't have enough room to take it in! Try it! Put me to the test!"*

— Malachi 3:10

What it comes down to is a practice of faith. An attitude of your heart. Put it on God. Test Him. He wants you to! The discipline of giving first — giving back to God what is His anyway — even if it's just a little, will reap a reward of plentifulness. This is the way to honor the Lord in your marriage by trusting Him with the resources He provides.

Give freely and become more wealthy; be stingy and lose everything. The generous will prosper; those who refresh others will themselves be refreshed.

— Proverbs 11:24–25

TAKE ACTION

- If you don't regularly give to the church, talk about starting an on-going, weekly giving plan.
- Read and discuss together Luke 6:38.

PRAY

Him: • Thank God for your job and His provisions.

Her: • Be honest with God and tell Him you are putting Him to the test with your faithful giving.

SAVING SMARTLY

Good planning and hard work lead to prosperity, but hasty shortcuts lead to poverty.

— Proverbs 21:5

The second area of financial success after giving is saving. Life has a way of surprising you with the unexpected. When it does, it's always good to have a cushion to fall back on. Some call it an Emergency Fund. Eventually, the car will need new tires, or some other maintenance upkeep. An unexpected trip to the doctor can result in some high costs. Or a child will need braces. An appliance will always break down at a most inconvenient time. Be prepared.

In Joseph's time, Egypt was able to survive a seven-year famine because Joseph instructed the people to save for seven years prior to the famine. He knew there would be a famine because the Lord told him. The time leading up to the fall-out was good in harvesting. But the people did as Joseph told them to do. When the famine hit, they not only survived, but were able to feed people in other lands as well (Genesis 41:41–57). I think that is brilliant financial wisdom! And it shows how God blesses those who are wise to save.

Even Paul told the Corinthians to save. "On the first day of each week, you should each put aside a portion of the money you have earned" (1 Corinthians 16:2).

Investing is a way of saving for the future. Jesus gave investment advice with the Parable Of The Talents in Matthew 25. There is a great reward for those who have been faithful in stewarding what God has placed in their hands.

Ants — they aren't strong, but they store up food all summer.

— Proverbs 30:25 (see also Proverbs 6:6–8)

Here are some things to remember about saving and investing:

- Get advice from others who know more than you.
- Only a fool doesn't plan ahead.
- It's good to save, invest and multiply your holdings.
- Don't forget to have diverse holdings in order to reduce risk.
- Invest in a way that's faithful to God's Word.
- Don't rely on money, rely on God.

Honor the Lord with all that He has given you as a marriage team. Glorify Him to the utmost in every word, deed and financial investment. Joyfully submit your portfolio to the Lord, for after all, everything belongs to Him. The maximum marriage handles its money smartly, leading to prosperity.

A wise man thinks ahead; a fool doesn't, and even brags about it!
— Proverbs 13:16

TAKE ACTION

- Just as you did for setting up a giving plan, set up a savings plan.

PRAY

Him:
- Thank God for the money you have in your possession right now.
- Thank God for His daily provisions.

Her:
- Ask God for ways to spend thriftily and save more.

SPENDING WISELY

The wise have wealth and luxury, but fools spend whatever they get.
— Proverbs 21:20

The third area of biblical financial success is spending. After you've given, and then put some away in savings, the thinking is now you can spend, spend, spend. You need just as much self-control and discipline here as you did with the giving and saving.

Notice that Solomon calls those a fool for spending everything. Plan your spending or you'll end up with nothing. Draw up a budget and stick to it as a couple and as a family. There's nothing wrong with spending money and enjoying the great things in life. It just needs to be done with wisdom and restraint.

If you start thinking to yourselves, "I did all this. And all by myself. I'm rich. It's all mine!" — well, think again. Remember that God, your God, gave you the strength to produce all this wealth so as to confirm the covenant that he promised to your ancestors — as it is today.
— Deuteronomy 8:17–18 (MSG)

If you have the mentality that you worked hard for this money, then you should be able to spend it how you please, you might be putting your love of money before your love of God. God still owns the amount in your bank account that's available for spending.

For the love of money is the root of all kinds of evil. And some people, craving money, have wandered from the true faith and pierced themselves with many sorrows.
— 1 Timothy 6:10

Being content is a necessary attitude of gratitude. In Luke 3:14 John said, "Be content with your wages." Benjamin Franklin said, "Contentment makes poor men rich; discontentment makes rich men poor." The writer of Hebrews says, "Make sure that your character is free from the love of money, being content with what you have; for He Himself has said, 'I will never desert you, nor will I ever forsake you...'" (Hebrews 13:5 NASB).

> "It is because God is with us always that we can say, 'I have found contentment.' No matter what happens, no one can take that from you. No one can take God's presence from you. And knowing that, you can face whatever comes your way in life. Maybe it will be the greatest challenge ever which will be difficult and hard. And maybe it will be untold blessings that would turn many a head. But you will be able to keep your balance in all of that, because you recognize that God is the provider. **Happiness and contentment do not come from stuff; they come from a relationship with God.**"*

The Lord is my shepherd; I have all that I need.
— Psalm 23:1

A maximum marriage couple is not focused on getting more, but is focused on being content with what God has already given them. They are grateful for having God as their provider and for their relationship with Him.

TAKE ACTION

- Read Philippians 4:11 and 4:19 and read a Study Bible notes for these verses.
- Make a budget together you both can live with.

PRAY

Him:
- Ask God for wisdom in spending your money wisely.
- Thank God for supplying your every need.

Her:
- Thank God for your many blessings that you tend to take for granted.
- Thank God for never leaving you.

*Greg Laurie Devotional, January 31, 2015, © 2019 Harvest Christian Fellowship

DESTROYING DEBT

Just as the rich rule the poor, so the borrower is servant to the lender.
— Proverbs 22:7

When you're in debt, you're in bondage. 1 Corinthians 7:21b says, "but if you get a chance to be free, take it." That is to say if you're in debt but you're able to get out of it, then by all means, do so. Being free from debt releases the bondage.

God's Word does not prohibit debt or say it's a sin. Yet everywhere it's mentioned, it is cast in a negative way. When you borrow, you become a servant to a bank, a business, or whoever you borrowed from by having to live under the terms of the loan. You are called to be servants to God alone.

Today's culture makes you believe you need more than you really need. Your neighbor has a nice car, why don't you? Reports indicate we consume twice as much material goods today as we did 50 years ago. Here are some reasons why we think we need more:

- We think having more gives us more security.
- We think having more will increase our happiness.
- We hope to impress people by our "wealth."
- We are actually jealous of those who have what we desire.
- We think having more will bring us confidence.
- We are more greedy and selfish than we like to admit.

Using a credit card for our purchases has become too easy. And many people have abused that situation. Credit card debt is revolving debt, which means that it's an open-ended line of credit. You can keep borrowing up to the amount of your credit limit as long as you keep paying your bill.

Revolving debt can easily be abused because you can carry a balance from month to month, and you just need to pay the minimum to keep going. This makes it easy for people to buy things they can't actually afford.

Non-revolving debt (also called installment debt), is borrowing for items which may include homes, cars, or student loans. Non-revolving debt means that there is a fixed amount borrowed and a pre-set plan to pay off the loan every month.*

Borrowing money to buy assets that appreciate in value and earn a rate of return is not the kind of borrowing that the Bible is warning about. If someone can borrow and create more wealth with the borrowed money, he could be considered a good steward of God's money. But one must be wise about all purchases.

Since everything is the Lord's, be extremely careful about going deep in debt, thereby becoming enslaved to the lender. Excess material possessions do not enrich our lives. Only God can truly give us enrichment. A maximum married couple will strive to serve God and trust in Him with their income.

TAKE ACTION

- If you have a problem with debt, look into programs such as Dave Ramsey's Financial Peace University (daveramsey.com) or Crown Financial Ministries (crown.org).

PRAY

Him:
- Ask God to give you control over your borrowing.
- Ask God for strength and discipline in destroying debt.

Her:
- Ask God for wisdom in borrowing wisely.
- Praise Him if you are debt-free!

*creditdonkey.com

TAKING CARE OF WHAT GOD HAS GIVEN YOU

The blessing of the L*ORD* *makes a person rich, and he adds no sorrow with it.*

— Proverbs 10:22

Regardless of how much money you have, it is by the blessing of God that you have any at all. C. S. Lewis says in *Mere Christianity*, "Every faculty you have, your power of thinking or moving your limbs from moment to moment, is given to you by God...you could not give Him anything that was not His own already." This includes how much money He has given you.

Your mindset should always be "God owns it all." As David says in Psalm 24:1, "The earth is the Lord's, and everything in it." And again in 1 Chronicles 29:14, "Everything we have has come from [God], ...we give [Him] only what [He] first gave us!" Author Bill Peel says, "Nothing is ours. Nothing really belongs to us. God owns everything; we're responsible for how we treat it and what we do with it."

Focus on managing *God's* resources, not your own. Thinking about money this way changes your perspective. You go from holding your money with a closed fist to holding it with an open hand. The irony is that the tighter you grip, the more likely you are to lose it all.

Concentrate on counting your blessings and you'll have little time to count anything else.

— Woodrow Kroll

It's not what you possess that makes you rich, it's only the blessings of the Lord. Having blessings doesn't always mean you have the most expensive house on the block, although God can bless you materially. God's favor will add immeasurable happiness to your life because He is the one who commands the blessing — thereby making your life enriched and abundant. No amount of hard work on our part will ever add to God's blessing or make it any better.

In your marriage relationship, an attitude of constant gratefulness for what God has given you is how your outlook on life should be. Seek unity in your marriage in how you manage your money and other blessings from God. You can maximize your joy in your lives by understanding and experiencing God's grace of bountiful blessings.

Teach those who are rich in this world not to be proud and not to trust in their money, which is so unreliable. Their trust should be in God, who richly gives us all we need for our enjoyment.

— 1 Timothy 6:17

TAKE ACTION

- Take an inventory of what God has given you — your health, your wealth, your joy.

PRAY

Him:
- Thank God for your home.
- Thank Him for allowing you to be a steward of all the things He has given you.

Her:
- Ask God to show you how to be a blessing to your husband.
- Thank God for the abundant life He has given you.

A Maximum Marriage DEMONSTRATES GENEROSITY

GIVING GENEROUSLY

[24]Give freely and become more wealthy; be stingy and lose everything. [25]The generous will prosper; those who refresh others will themselves be refreshed.

— Proverbs 11:24–25

How do you practice generosity in your marriage? Generosity can have a variety of meanings. It can mean how you share your money. It can mean how you share your time with each other. It can mean using your God-given talents to help others.

Since being generous with your money was written about on pages 144–145, I'll explore here how to be generous with each other to maximize your marriage. Thinking about being generous with your spouse is being unselfish, big-hearted, kind, and self-sacrificing. Looking at this Proverb from the married perspective reveals a lavish setting if generosity is practiced.

Give freely.

To the one who gives freely, there is no holding back. You are giving your all to your spouse without hoping to get something in return. I think it would be safe to say most of us don't like housework chores. Yet when I vacuum the house releasing my wife of this responsibility, she is blessed by my act of kindness. If you give without griping, you will have a more comfortable environment, or you'll be, in a sense, wealthy.

Don't be stingy.

You can't give freely and be stingy at the same time. Being stingy is being selfish. If I don't want to be attentive or give of my time to my wife, I am being mean. Here Solomon tells us being close-fisted in this manner will result in losing everything. However long you have been married, you can lose everything you've built just by being selfish. I believe most divorces are caused by selfishness.

The generous will prosper.

On the other hand, see how verse 25 shows us what we all desire — a flourishing marriage. Building a maximum marriage requires being generous with your kindness. The couple who are generous to each other are the thriving couple.

Refresh others.

Don't you enjoy it when someone does something nice for you? It re-energizes you. It picks you up. So refresh your spouse by giving generously to their needs. The great thing about doing so, you'll be re-energized as well. 2 Corinthians 9:6 says, "Whoever sows sparingly will also reap sparingly, and whoever sows generously will also reap generously." This verse can be applied to finances, but it can also be applied to a relational connection. Refreshing your spouse results in refreshing yourself.

Give generously to each other for a prosperous marriage.

TAKE ACTION

- Use the list of blessings on the following pages for ideas on how to be generous with each other. Make a point to bless each other every day.

PRAY

Him:
- Thank God for a flourishing marriage.
- Ask God to show you how to spread more kindness.

Her:
- Ask God to pour more of Himself into you so you can pour out to your husband and family.

A list of blessings (random acts of kindness) to share with your spouse.

1. Buy your spouse their favorite piece of chocolate, place it on their pillow, and write a love note.
2. Take a short walk, hold hands, and talk about a happy memory.
3. Use hand lotion and give your spouse a hand or foot massage.
4. Send your spouse a love text.
5. Surprise your spouse with their favorite drink for no reason.
6. Help your spouse with dinner and the dishes.
7. Write a love note on the bathroom mirror with a dry erase marker.
8. Complete an errand for them.
9. Take your spouse's car and fill it with gas and have it washed.
10. Have some friends over for playing a game.
11. Tell your spouse how proud you are of them on completing a certain task.
12. Take a Sunday afternoon drive.
13. Spend an evening together watching an old movie.
14. Prepare a romantic dinner, with candles on the table.
15. Tell a funny memory that always makes both of you laugh.
16. Snuggle together on the couch.
17. Go get an ice cream together.
18. Send your spouse a love letter in the mail.
19. Make a date to see lights in your town or drive around in an expensive neighborhood and gawk at the houses.
20. Do one thing to make your spouse's day easier.
21. Turn the bed down for your spouse and place a mint on their pillow.
22. Tackle a small project together.
23. Go out for coffee together and talk about a vacation.
24. Plan a double-date with another couple.
25. Look for a Netflix series to get interested in together. With popcorn!
26. Ask your spouse what was the best thing that happened to them during their day.
27. Order your favorite meal at your favorite restaurant to "take-out," if possible.
28. Write a love message on a sticky-note and leave it in their underwear drawer.
29. Bring coffee to your spouse before they get out of bed.
30. Give your spouse a shoulder rub.
31. Offer to clean the dishes after dinner.

32. Ask your spouse what their favorite book was and why.
33. Play a card game with just the two of you.
34. Go window shopping.
35. Buy your spouse a "just because" card.
36. Make your spouse's favorite dessert.
37. Complete a task on the "Honey-Do" list.
38. Let the "Honey-Do" list slide for a few days.
39. Complete a chore that is difficult for your spouse to do.
40. Put the children to bed if you're not the usual one to do this.
41. Take the children out to allow some "alone time" for your spouse.
42. Run a bubble bath for your spouse.
43. Give flowers for no reason.
44. Ask how you can pray for your spouse for their day.
45. Vacuum the house or their car.
46. Call your spouse at work, just because you thought about them.
47. Clean and straighten your spouse's closest.
48. Choose a special day to say nothing but positive things that you like about your spouse.
49. Make your spouse a late night snack.
50. Share with friends a funny dating story that happened to you.
51. Organize your spouse's drawers.
52. Plan a picnic.
53. Put on some romantic music and cuddle or dance.
54. Get a hotel for a weekend in town or in a nearby town.
55. Tell your spouse that if you had the choice, you'd marry them again.
56. Watch your spouse's favorite sport or movie, even if you don't care for it.
57. Hug for no reason.
58. Reach out and touch the other for no reason and smile at them.
59. Kiss for no reason, and make it an extended one.
60. Play your spouse's favorite music.
61. Shoot silly selfies.
62. Leave a love note in your spouse's car.
63. Turn off the TV for a night and talk about future trips or dreams.
64. Make an effort to do something that really pleases your spouse.
65. Say, "Thank You!"
66. Compliment your spouse on their appearance.

DO IT NOW

Do not withhold good from those who deserve it when it's in your power to help them. If you can help your neighbor now, don't say, "Come back tomorrow, and then I'll help you."

— Proverbs 3:27–28

There's a joke about marriage that says, "Ladies, if your husband said he's going to fix something, he will do it. There's no need to remind him every 6 months." Unfortunately, this is more of an insult to men rather than to the nagging wife. When it's convenient in the man's mind, he'll get to the project. This creates an inconvenience to the wife.

What's interesting about this Proverb is that it can correlate to paying your personal debts as well as helping others in need. Since we're not dwelling on monetary generosity in this section, we'll study these verses on being generous in your deeds. From both the husband's and the wife's viewpoints. Your spouse is your closest neighbor.

Remember when you fell in love with each other? Wouldn't you admit that your spouse is deserving of loving actions from you? Using an excuse such as "They know I love them" is a cop-out. Love is an action verb. Show them! When you dated, you probably did things almost unconsciously that proved your commitment to the relationship.

Husbands, *since* your wife is deserving, and you have the power to do good things for her benefit and convenience, do it! If your wife is continually making a "honey-do" list, you might believe you are being controlled. On the contrary, she is wanting you to demonstrate your man-power and expertise in accomplishing the list. By completing her requests, you are saying "I love you" without even voicing it. And there's a reason she brings up a task. It's important to her in the moment. So don't wait for a better time when your schedule is more open. If it's not convenient, let her know your reasoning and give her a definite timetable when you think you can get to it.

Wives, *since* your husband is deserving, Solomon says don't withhold good from him. When you have the ability to bless him with something he desires, do it! Yes, this can mean making love. It can also mean cooking his favorite meal. It can mean doing whatever he likes, but what you don't necessarily desire to do in the moment, yet you have the ability to do so. Withholding anything delays blessing him, thereby delaying the blessing you would receive in return.

Love one another with brotherly affection. Outdo one another in showing honor.

— Romans 12:10 (ESV)

Don't make excuses and hope that your spouse's requests will be forgotten eventually. Telling someone to go and come another time is a cover for selfishness. Generous couples give of themselves willingly. Today is the time of need! Not tomorrow! The blessing of a delayed action is watered down. Keep the blessing fresh. See how Paul describes the harvest you'll reap:

So let's not get tired of doing what is good. At just the right time we will reap a harvest of blessing if we don't give up. Therefore, whenever we have the opportunity, we should do good to everyone — especially to those in the family of faith.

— Galatians 6:9–10

TAKE ACTION

- If your spouse has asked you to do something for them and you haven't gotten around to it, apologize now and put it on your calendar. Now.

PRAY

Him: • Thank God for opportunities to do good things for your wife.

Her: • Thank God for being able to daily express your love to your deserving husband.

GIFTING MAKES THE TEAM STRONGER

A gift opens the way and ushers the giver into the presence of the great.
— Proverbs 18:16 (NIV)

The beauty of God's Word is that it can often be approached from different perspectives. This Proverb at first glance could be referring to the ancient culture of bringing gifts to others when they showed hospitality to you. In doing so, you would be exalted. It's a simple recognition of fact: generosity and politeness open many doors.

Let's look at this verse from the perspective of marriage. A husband and wife each bring their own gifts, or skills, into their relationship. God has given each of them a unique ability for the sole purpose of glorifying Him. Romans 12:6 says, "In his grace, God has given us different gifts for doing certain things well."

There are many aspects in your marriage where identifying your strengths and deciding pro-actively who is best suited to handle certain tasks will be beneficial. Understand that you each have weaknesses and strengths. Where you may be weak in one area is where your spouse may be strong. And vice versa. It is vital to respect each other's differences. It's what makes you a team.

It's not until you see your spouse's strengths as unique yet equally as powerful as yours that you can mutually submit and live in a shared balance of power.
— Jimmy Evans & Allan Kelsey, *Strengths Based Marriage**

Each of you should use whatever gift you have received to serve others.
— 1 Peter 4:10

There have been multiple studies that have proven where those who said their spouse showed frequent generosity were also the happiest in their marriages. This only follows what Jesus modeled. We are

**Strengths Based Marriage* © 2016 by Jimmy Evans and Allan Kelsey, Thomas Nelson, Nashville, TN here to serve others, especially our spouses. When you demonstrate your God-given skills within your marriage, you are serving in the manner that God intended.

Here are three ways to increase generosity in your marriage:

1. **Show gratitude.** When your spouse executes his gift, or strength, acknowledge it and thank them for it.
2. **Express love.** In a generous marriage, spouses regularly show and tell each other that the other is noticed, cared for, and valued.
3. **Share acts of kindness.** Instead of doing what you would want, put yourself in your spouse's shoes and ask: "What would he or she like?" Then do it.

Kindness and purposeful generosity act like super glue in marriage. Gift each other with these attributes and you'll be in the presence of greatness.

You will be enriched in every way so that you can be generous on every occasion…your generosity will result in thanksgiving to God.
— 2 Corinthians 9:11

TAKE ACTION

- Discuss what things you're both good at, and especially what things you really enjoy. These may be your gifts.
- Read 1 Corinthians 12 and discuss each other's gifts and how you can use them within your marriage and towards others.
- Say "Thank you," express love, and do an act of kindness.

PRAY

Him:
- Ask God for ways to fulfill your gifts to your wife.
- Thank Him for giving you your abilities and skills.

Her:
- Ask God to help you use your strengths and to be understanding regarding your weaknesses.
- Thank God for your gifts.

EMBRACING EACH OTHER

Let your wife be a fountain of blessing for you. Rejoice in the wife of your youth.

— Proverbs 5:18

Solomon wrote an entire book about marital sexuality in Song of Songs. However, in Proverbs, he spends much of the time teaching the importance of avoiding infidelity. We will pursue fidelity in this section. The pitfalls of infidelity will be studied in pages 166–169.

The entire fifth chapter of Proverbs is about avoiding the immoral woman (but also could be substituted for an immoral man). In verse 18 he reminds the husband of the importance of accepting your wife as a gift from God (see page 18 on viewing your spouse as a gift). This verse can be summed up in three words: embrace your wife! Or embrace your husband!

God created sex, so therefore it is good. The world has corrupted it and made it bad. Pursuing sexual satisfaction within marriage is God's plan. You honor God by engaging in this gift. "A fountain of blessing" describes unabashedly to seek fulfillment of sexual intimacy only from your wife. Desires that spring up are to be rightly fostered for the enjoyment and good of both the husband and wife, but only within the institution of marriage.

In the previous verses (15–17) he further describes the imagery of fountains.

> 15 "Drink water from your own well —
> share your love only with your wife.
> 16 Why spill the water of your springs in the streets,
> having sex with just anyone?
> 17 You should reserve it for yourselves.
> Never share it with strangers."

A "well" and "spring" are metaphors for a sexually excited woman and man, respectively. (Yes, the Bible can be sexy!) The possessive pronoun "your" indicates that the wife's body belongs to her husband. In 1 Corinthians 7:4, the Apostle Paul concurs with this statement that the husband's body also belongs to the wife. Marriage is thus a matter of mutual possession. And it is an exclusive, private party. Sexual intimacy between spouses is never to be shared with others.

You are my private garden, my treasure, my bride, a secluded spring, a hidden fountain.

— Song of Songs 4:12

Marital sexuality is supposed to be a matter of blessedness, joy, satisfaction, and captivation to both of you. And it should continue throughout your lifetime. Solomon encourages men to seek joy "in the wife of your youth." The same could be said for wives to enjoy the husbands of their youth. Rejoice means to be jubilant, ecstatic, in seventh heaven, over the moon, on cloud nine. Finding real joy and satisfaction is delighting in your gift from God throughout the years!

TAKE ACTION

- Perhaps "take action" is self-explanatory…
- Read Song of Songs together — possibly one chapter per day, along with a Christian-based study guide.

PRAY

Him:
- Thank God for your wife!
- Express to God how ecstatic you are about her.
- Thank God for the beauty of making love.

Her:
- Thank God for your husband!
- Express to God how "over the moon" your desire is of your husband.
- Thank God for the beauty of making love.

DELIGHTING IN THE PHYSICAL

[She is] a lovely deer, a graceful doe. Let her breasts fill you at all times with delight; be intoxicated always in her love.

— Proverbs 5:19 (ESV)

Solomon gives us three important choices to make in this God-inspired verse. First, a husband should cherish his wife tenderly as a delicate object of affection. Second, he should appreciate *only* her body and sexuality. And third, he should let her affection and devotion consume him.

In Solomon's time, female deer were tamed and enjoyed as pets. He also refers to them in describing a wife's beauty in Song of Songs 4:5 and 7:3. As you think about deer, you understand they are delicate and graceful, and you would certainly treat them in a loving and pleasant way — the way you should treat your wife. Paul also confirmed this aspect of treatment in Ephesians 5:28–29, when he commands husbands to cherish — treat with special care — their wives. And again in Colossians:

Husbands, love your wives and never treat them harshly.

— Colossians 3:19

While breasts are mentioned specifically here, this can imply a figure of speech representing the entire body, and of sexual pleasure. Husbands and wives should learn to enjoy each others' bodies to the fullest for maximum intimacy. At all times!

Julie Sibert, speaker and writer on sexual intimacy, says, "I think the more confident, intentional, and generous a husband and wife grow in their sexual intimacy, the easier it is for them to see God's provision in intimacy. God could have downplayed or left out all together the potential for breasts to be erogenous, relegating them nothing beyond sustenance for a baby. But He is a God of abundance. And just as sex is for more than just procreation, the various features of our body are well designed for more too."*

To be intoxicated in her love means to be totally invigorated. Other translations use words such as "ravished," "captivated," "exhilarated," "infatuated," and "be lost." The command here is for complete marital fidelity. Always! Being totally consumed with your wife will help you eliminate the chances of infidelity ever happening.

Husband, the advice is simple: consider and treat her delicately with tender affection. Choose to be always satisfied with her body and lovemaking. Focus on her devotion, love, and loyalty. Then you will be immensely happy!

Wife, if your husband is to be satisfied, even ravished, with you in the three ways described here for a maximum marriage, you have a tremendous responsibility. You are to be a delicate and gracious woman deserving affection. Take care that you are always attractive and alluring.

God wants you to enjoy each other physically and to be content. The sexual union of a husband and wife is a holy merger.

Love each other with genuine affection, and take delight in honoring each other.

— Romans 12:10

▒ TAKE ACTION

- Indulge in each other.

▒ PRAY

Him: • Thank God for your beautiful wife and the gift of sex.

Her: • Thank God for your admiring husband and the gift of sex.

---

*© 2019, Julie Sibert. Intimacyinmarriage.com

RUNNING FROM IMMORALITY

16Wisdom will save you from the immoral woman, from the seductive words of the promiscuous woman. 17She has abandoned her husband and ignores the covenant she made before God. 18Entering her house leads to death; it is the road to the grave. 19The man who visits her is doomed. He will never reach the paths of life.

— Proverbs 2:16–19

Solomon devotes large segments of his book of wisdom to avoiding the pitfalls of immorality (See also Proverbs 5:1–20; 6:24–29; and the entire 7th chapter). These warnings are not just for men to avoid adultery, but for all believers — men and women — not to be enticed by the empty promises of sinful pleasures.

The other large segments of his book are devoted to pursuing wisdom. It is through wisdom that you can recognize danger and knowing when to say no to temptations. He uses the imagery of a seductive woman to help all of us recognize the signs of manipulation by fleshly desires. These signs are as follows:

1. The immoral person has flattering and enticing words, which those who desire to be godly must learn to ignore (Prov. 2:16). Persuasive and appealing speech will doom those looking for exactly that kind of affirmation.

...Her mouth is smoother than oil.

— Proverbs 5:3

2. The immoral person has chosen to ignore what God has said and also to forget certain promises made to Him (Prov. 2:17). A Christian marriage ceremony consecrates the union of a man and a woman as *holy* in God's eyes. This bond between a husband and wife supersedes all other relationships. Immorality shuns God's holy design.

Give honor to marriage and remain faithful to one another in marriage.
— Hebrews 13:4

3. The immoral person dresses in promiscuous clothing (Prov. 7:10). Any attire that can be interpreted or designed to stimulate sexual desire is wrong.*

Infidelity will always lead to destruction. Never think you can get away with it, or that it won't hurt anyone. Read again Proverbs 2:18–19. You can avoid the wreckage by consuming God's wisdom.

If you have fallen, remember that God is always faithful, filled with loving forgiveness. He can restore you and give you a renewed purity. You only need to trust Him. He answered David's prayer to create within him a clean heart (Psalm 51:10) when he fell in adultery. Because God even said of David, "I have found a man after my own heart" (Acts 13:22).

A maximum marriage pursues God's wisdom so that the husband and wife recognize evil that attempts to take away their holy union.

TAKE ACTION

- Read Genesis 2:24. Discuss forgiveness if there is broken vows.

PRAY

Him: • Ask God to create within you a clean heart and a strong desire to pursue His holiness.

Her: • Ask God to give you a strong sense of devotedness to your husband and to pursue God's holiness in all your actions.

---

*From the *Swindoll Study Bible*, p. 747, an edition of the *Holy Bible*, New Living Translation, copyright © 1996, 2004, 2015 by Tyndale House Foundation. Used by permission of Tyndale House Publishers, Inc., Carol Stream, Illinois 60188. All rights reserved.

KEEPING YOUR HEART FROM STRAYING

[24]So listen to me, my sons, and pay attention to my words. [25]Don't let your hearts stray away toward her. Don't wander down her wayward path. [26]For she has been the ruin of many; many men have been her victims. [27]Her house is the road to the grave. Her bedroom is the den of death.

— Proverbs 7:24–27

Listen! Pay attention! These are strong words Solomon uses stressing the importance of what he is trying to convey. Notice also the words "stray" and "wander." When you think of someone straying or wandering, they are lost, sidetracked, and off course. These are powerful warnings to us all — men and women.

I want to turn your thinking around on this. What if "immoral woman" was replaced throughout these scriptures with the word "pornography." For instance, Proverbs 2:19 would read, "The man who visits pornography is doomed." And Proverbs 5:8, "Stay away from porn!"

While you may think you would never engage in the actual act of infidelity, Jesus hits you in the gut when he said if you even lust after someone else, you've committed adultery (Matthew 5:28). Therefore, viewing porn is adultery. For men *and* women. And women, explicit novels can be considered immoral and pornographic.

Now read Proverbs 5:3–14 and see the destruction this brings. You will lose your honor. Strangers will consume your money. You'll groan in anguish and get sickly. You will face utter ruin and public disgrace. In Proverbs 7:22–23, you are like an ox going to slaughter. You're a deer caught in a trap; a bird flying into a snare.

Look how Proverbs 6:25–28 in *The Message* translation reads in this regard: "Don't lustfully fantasize on her beauty, nor be taken in by her bedroom eyes. You can buy an hour with a whore for a loaf of bread, but a wanton woman may well eat you alive. Can you build a fire in your lap and not burn your pants? Can you walk barefoot on hot coals and not get blisters?" Solomon is extremely concerned that you don't get burned! It sounds like to me he is trying to scare you straight. Be careful!

He will die for lack of self-control; he will be lost because of his great foolishness.

— Proverbs 5:23

How can you handle the savage assault of this alluring intruder? When temptation comes, and it will, yell out to Satan to get out of here! Hold on to God as your shield and warrior. Take on His armor (Ephesians 6:13–17). Remember that Christ's death and resurrection freed you from sin's dominion and gave you a new Master! No matter how persistently this thing attacks, the power of Jesus within you can slam the door in its face. You can say, "NO!" over and over again, and it will back off.

Solomon concurs in Proverbs 6:24, "[The wisdom of the LORD] will keep you from [pornography]." Stay on track with your devotion to the Lord, and you and your marriage relationship will thrive.

I will lead a life of integrity in my own home. I will refuse to look at anything vile and vulgar.

— Psalm 101:2b–3

TAKE ACTION

- Take corrective action that you don't go near the fire in any way. Wives, help your husbands in this regard with a loving, forgiving heart. Husbands, really devote yourselves to your wives (Prov. 5:15–19, see page 162).

PRAY

Him: • Pray Psalm 101.

Her: • In the name of Jesus Christ, demand that Satan would be destroyed in this area for the sake of your marriage.

STAYING ON TRACK

Look straight ahead, and fix your eyes on what lies before you. Mark out a straight path for your feet; stay on the safe path. Don't get sidetracked; keep your feet from following evil.

— Proverbs 4:25–27

This thing called marriage can be an adventurous, often treacherous, journey. There will always be rough roads in this expedition. Jesus assured us of that in John 16:33. He never promises us Disneyland or smooth sailing. But there is a pathway that assures safety.

Fix your eyes.

Blinders are used on horses to stop them from being distracted and keeping them pointed in the direction they are supposed to be headed. The blinders cover the rear vision of the horse, forcing it to look only in a forward direction and keeping it on track.

We would look silly with blinders on but we are prone to wander. This world will do everything it can to get you off track. Set your eyes on being devoted to serving God and your spouse each day.

Mark out a straight path.

It is the duty of every Christian to prove everything he does by the Word of God and reject any contrary opinion or activity (1 Thessalonians 5:21). You cannot get to a desired destination without first identifying the direction you should take. If you want a long-lasting marriage, map out the route to get there, and then go! The Bible is the best GPS navigation system out there.

Keep your feet.

Headlights shine straight ahead to show you the road (that's why they're called *head*lights). Getting sidetracked puts you on a crooked road. Getting off track will always be a derailment and a train wreck. Watch where you plant your feet.

Your word is a lamp to guide my feet and a light for my path.
— Psalm 119:105

The way of a maximum marriage — the road to happiness and faithfulness — is straight. Do not turn even a little. Devote yourselves to God's Word.

> There are roads that take you everywhere, but where you need to go.
> There are roads that don't go anywhere, and one that leads you home.
> The way is rough and steep; it is the path to the one I seek,
> And I must go on.
> I'll follow in the path of the man with the nail scars in his hands.*

TAKE ACTION

- Study Proverbs 2:20 and Proverbs 3:5–6 (See page 20). Discuss how you might improve your spiritual walk, individually and together.

PRAY

Him:
- Ask God to afix your eyes on Him at all times, in everything you do.
- Thank God for showing you direction in your marriage.

Her:
- Ask God to put "blinders" on your eyes to the world's crooked roads, so that you can focus on His straight and narrow ways, with understanding they lead to joy.

* "The Man With The Nail Scars," David Meece, 1989

KEEPING GOOD COMPANY

My child, if sinners entice you, turn your back on them! Don't go along with them! Stay far away from their paths.

— Proverbs 1:10; 15

Remember when Jesus was tempted by Satan in Matthew 4:1–11? Satan did all he could to entice Jesus into serving him. But in verse 10, Jesus essentially turns his back on Satan. "Jesus' refusal was curt: 'Beat it, Satan!' He backed his rebuke with a quotation from Deuteronomy: 'Worship the Lord your God, and only him. Serve him with absolute single-heartedness'" (THE MESSAGE).

Then in Matthew 16:23, Jesus turns his back on Peter. "But He turned and said to Peter, 'Get behind Me, Satan! You are an offense to Me, for you are not mindful of the things of God, but the things of men'" (NKJV). The context here is that Peter was suggesting that Jesus take a course of action other than the one that He was predestined to fulfill — death on the cross. Jesus knew His destiny, and he knew the will of the Father. What Peter was suggesting was that Jesus go against the will of the Father.

The word translated "Satan" here means "adversary."As such, Peter's words were the words of an adversary of God. Surely, Peter loved Jesus, he just didn't want to see Him die. Nonetheless, his suggestion was in direct opposition to the will of God.

Do not be deceived: Bad company ruins good morals.

— 1 Corinthians 15:33 (ESV)

It's really hard to follow someone whom you've turn your back on. It's also really hard to even see what they're doing. Don't fail to notice the exclamation points in today's Proverb. Solomon is emphasizing this importance. Surrounding yourself with good quality Christian friends is essential for staying on the path of moral living.

In verses 10–18 of this first chapter in Proverbs, Solomon goes into detail about what immoral people do. Even birds know to stay away when they see a trap (v. 17).

As a couple, stay on the straight path and focus on keeping Jesus in front of you. Keep company with other couples who build you up spiritually and morally. You can easily do this by attending church regularly or engaging in a group Bible study.

Don't you realize that friendship with the world makes you an enemy of God? I say it again: If you want to be a friend of the world, you make yourself an enemy of God.

— James 4:4

Walk with the wise and become wise; associate with fools and get in trouble.

— Proverbs 13:20

TAKE ACTION

- Read Matthew 4:1–11 and discuss the techniques that Christ uses to stay moral and pure.

PRAY

Him: • Pray in the name of Jesus Christ for Satan to "Beat it!" in your marriage. Ask for God to protect you with angels that will safeguard you from immoral people, and from being influenced by them, and He will.

Her: • Thank God for your spiritual friends. Ask Him to give you more.

PROTECTED ON ALL SIDES

The Lord is a shield to those who walk with integrity. He guards the paths of the just and protects those who are faithful to him.
— Proverbs 2:7b–8

I'll never forget that drive along the Kahekili Highway in Maui on our Hawaiian vacation. First, I'm in a rental car that I'm not used to driving. Second, the road is mainly a narrow, curvy, mountainous cliff-hugging, one-lane route without guardrails! There are occasional pullouts if a car is coming from the opposite direction. Later, we found out driving on this road violated our rental car agreement. They didn't want us on that road. The views were spectacular, but I could hardly enjoy them because of the lack of protection from the sheer drop-off.

How wonderful to have One who puts guardrails on our pathways in life! When you walk with the Lord, He promises protection. There are boundaries in the godly life. If you go outside the lines, you'll most likely fall.

Notice the prerequisites of this protection: having integrity, being just, and being faithful.

Solomon mentions walking in integrity multiple times in his book and it's mentioned elsewhere throughout the Bible. But how do you walk in integrity? (See also page 180) Simply put, it means being totally honest. As well as keeping your promises. Zig Ziglar said, "With integrity, you have nothing to fear, since you have nothing to hide. With integrity, you will do the right thing, so you will have no guilt."

Whoever walks in integrity will be delivered, but he who is crooked in his ways will suddenly fall.
— Proverbs 28:18 (See also Proverbs 10:9)

What does it mean to be just? To be just means to be honorable and fair in your dealings with other people; to be consistent with what is morally right. Also, to be just means to have a good character and good morals. A right relationship with God defines a just person.

Those who follow the right path fear the LORD; those who take the wrong path despise him.

— Proverbs 14:2

Being faithful is having a constant, devoted loyalty. God is always faithful to you. "But you, O Lord, are a God of compassion and mercy, slow to get angry and filled with unfailing love and faithfulness" (Psalm 86:15). The Bible clearly shows that faith is not just a one-time decision to follow Christ but we are called to increase in faith. Faith has been described like a muscle. Not using a muscle will cause it to wither and become weak. Your faith is the same way. You need to use your faith muscle continually and grow to be like Christ.

A faithful man will abound with blessings….

— Proverbs 28:20

Marriage partners walking justly, faithfully, and with integrity will be guarded and protected. Therefore, you can count on God's faithfulness to maximize your relationship with each other. What a blessing to go through life with God guarding your side!

TAKE ACTION

- Read Psalm 91 and 121. Or pray them.

PRAY

Him:

- Ask God to increase your faith today.
- Ask God to strengthen your resolve to walk in integrity.
- Thank God for His daily protection and faithfulness.

Her:

- Ask God to cultivate a love within you to live in integrity.
- Thank God for being your Guard, your Shield, and your Protector.

SEIZING THE DAY

A lazy person's way is blocked with briars, but the path of the upright is an open highway.

— Proverbs 15:19

Each day you have a choice. You can choose to follow God's pathway or choose not to. Who wouldn't want to see nothing but open highway ahead of them? Zooming along, hair blowing in the wind, and enjoying the journey!

Contrary to following God's highway of life is the lazy person. His way is filled with briars, or as I would call them, excuses. Briars have prickly thorns. If you saw your way blocked by those, you'd probably not want to proceed at all. Excuses often keep you from proceeding towards the place where God desires you to be.

We all make excuses from time to time. It's an attempt to lessen the blame or a way to justify our faults. In your marriage, excuses will keep you from getting to maximum heights. Let's look at five excuses that will keep you from that open highway.

Excuse #1: Things aren't that bad. Within this mentality is mediocrity. What you're really saying is you don't need to improve.

Excuse #2: We can fix it on our own. Those who think along these lines believe seeking advice is an admission of weakness or defeat — "Only those who have severe issues need outside help." That's bad thinking.

Excuse #3: All the problems are your spouse's fault. Blame shift. It's been happening since the beginning of time, when Adam told God it was the woman He gave him that made him fall. If you don't believe you might be part of the problem, then it'll be impossible to believe you can be part of the solution.

Excuse #4: I don't need to change, my spouse does. Change can be difficult and uncomfortable. If you do what you've always done, you won't get ahead. The reality is only *you* can change you.

Excuse #5: You don't want to admit failure. Of course, nobody likes to admit failure. Couples can actually avoid getting help to save their crumbling marriage in order to *not* feel like failures. Outside help, whether it's a professional counselor or older Christian mentor couple, is the pathway to success.

I attribute my success to this — I never gave or took any excuse.
— Florence Nightingale

It is easier to move from failure to success than from excuses to success.
— John C. Maxwell

Perhaps it's time to prune the briars, to cut those thorns off that have kept you from seeing the open highway. Seize the day to drive down God's open highway of a fulfilled married life. Enjoy the ride!

TAKE ACTION

- Does it feel like you're walking through the briar patch? Do some inventory on your spiritual walk. Are you studying your Bible? Could you pray more often? Throw out the excuses. They come from Satan himself. Ask your spouse to help you improve in the areas of spiritual lack. Blessings of an open highway will surely follow obedience.

PRAY

Him:
- Ask God to help you see your own excuses and to destroy them.
- Thank God for giving you joy in an open highway.

Her:
- Ask God for insight where you have lacked spiritually and ask for guidance in establishing better habits in walking closer to Him day by day.

POINTED PARENTING, Part 1

Direct your children onto the right path, and when they are older, they will not leave it.

— Proverbs 22:6

There is probably no greater verse than this one on the powerful responsibility parents have in raising children. It is important to understand this is not a guarantee. God gave each person a free will and many a Christian parent has felt the pain of a child who turned from the faith. It is however, a *guide* for parenting in a godly home.

Charles Swindoll explains his amplified rendering of this verse this way: "Train your children in keeping with their individual gifts and bents, understanding the God-given abilities and characteristics they're born with as well as their particular tendencies toward evil and rebellion, and when they come to maturity, they will know who they are and therefore will not turn aside from the training they have received."

As long as your children are living under your roof, you are to train, to discipline, to instruct, to dedicate their lives to spiritual living. Your job is to cultivate an appetite for a godly life by your example.

The "right path" is not a career path you desire for them. You cannot force them to live up to your dreams because God has given them unique personalities and talents. Point out the wisdom of various God-honoring paths they might choose, and then let them choose. This will help develop their own character.

Foolishness is bound up in the heart of a child; Correction administered with godly wisdom and lovingkindness will remove it far from him.

— Proverbs 22:15 (AMP)

What is the advantage of raising children in a godly home? First, it makes a more pleasant and peaceful environment to have children trained in love, respect, obedience, kindness, etc. It is in stark contrast to homes in which children do whatever they please at all times!

But more than that, parents rearing their children in a godly manner give those children a beautiful example of what it would mean for them to choose God's way of life — when the time comes for them to make a choice. Children in a home managed by godly parents will have the opportunity to see God's way of life in action year after year. When the children reach maturity, they will then have a better understanding of the consequences or rewards that will come from their choices.

The home should be a self-contained shelter of security, a kind of school where life's basic lessons are taught, and a kind of church where God is honored.
— Billy Graham

Children watch their parents and will choose to model their lives or choose not to. It's therefore essential that the husband loves his wife and models God's design of a godly marriage. Parents cannot train their children to walk godly ways if they are not walking the same way. A maximum marriage models authentic love so the child can see God's love in their relationship.

TAKE ACTION

- Discuss how you can raise your children in showing love, respect, obedience, and kindness. Model those with strong ethics in the way of attending church regularly, praying with them, and discussing the Bible.

PRAY

Him:
- Ask God for the wisdom in instructing your children in the right way.
- Ask God to guide your children into making the right choices in their lives.

Her:
- Pray earnestly that your children will always be surrounded by godly friends.

☐☐ **POINTED PARENTING, Part 2**

The godly walk with integrity; blessed are their children who follow them.

— Proverbs 20:7

Simply put, walking with integrity will bless your children. But that's a tall order! What does it mean to walk with integrity?

Integrity is the quality of being honest and having strong moral principles — walking a godly path. It means you do what you say you're going to do. It doesn't mean you're perfect, but you're willing to admit your shortcomings. You own up to mistakes that are made and make amends where necessary.

Here are some steps in how to walk with integrity:

1. **Pursue a love for it.** A personal passion and love for integrity is the greatest motivation and drive for achieving it.
2. **Contemplate the blessings of it.** Investing in the time, energy, and money to be a good example for your kids, will empower you to make the daily choices and sacrifices that'll take you further along the path of integrity.
3. **Surround yourself with friends of integrity.** Having friends of impeccable integrity, righteousness, sincerity, and honesty, and spending time with them, influences your walk.
4. **Seek God's help.** It's a difficult choice to walk with integrity. In those times when you want to give up, ask the help of God through prayer. He will strengthen you with the power of His Spirit.

The LORD *directs the steps of the godly. He delights in every detail of their lives.*

— Psalm 37:23

As integrity encompasses your very being, your children will follow. I believe every parent wants the best for their children. It starts with you — you have to be at your very best. See how Charles Swindoll describes this important virtue:

> "When it comes to 'training up the child in the way he should go,' you've got the inside lane, Mom and Dad. So—take it easy! Remember (as Anne Ortlund puts it) 'children are wet cement.' They take the shape of your mold. They're learning even when you don't think they're watching. And those little guys and gals are plenty smart. They hear tone as well as terms. They read looks as well as books. They figure out motives, even those you think you can hide. They are not fooled, not in the long haul.
>
> "The two most important tools of parenting are time and touch. Believe me, both are essential. If you and I hope to release from our nest fairly capable and relatively stable people who can soar and make it on their own, we'll need to pay the price of saying no to many of our own wants and needs in order to interact with our young... and we'll have to keep breaking down the distance that only naturally forms as our little people grow up."*

A godly Mom and Dad walking in strong moral principles is the best environment and example for children to walk under.

TAKE ACTION

- Show your children, grandchildren, or other children what integrity looks like by living a moral life.

PRAY

Him:
- Ask God for a passion for integrity for your kids' sake.
- Thank God for your godly friends.

Her:
- Thank God for the blessings of sacrificing for your children.
- Ask God to give you strength through the struggles of raising children.

---

*Taken from *Day by Day with Charles Swindoll* by Charles R. Swindoll. Copyright © 2000 by Charles R. Swindoll, Inc. Thomas Nelson, Nashville, TN

ACHIEVING THE BLESSED HOME, Part 1

The Lord *curses the house of the wicked, but he blesses the home of the upright.*

— Proverbs 3:33b

Would you want to live in a house under a curse? I seriously doubt it. And you probably don't even like to talk about curses because you may think they are Satanic evil. A curse of God is not a curse in the sense of an evil spell, but simply the judgment of God upon sin.

All true curses in the Bible were brought on by God or in behalf of God by His prophets or apostles. This is very important. Satan and demons are real and they are working against believers, but no curse is attributed to Satan anywhere in the Bible. So there is, in fact, no such thing as a Satanic or demonic curse.

From the beginning, man has been under a curse. The fall of Adam (Genesis 3:14–17) caused this curse of death by God due to man's sin, and it continues from generation to generation. Because we've all sinned, we're under a curse.

Paul tells us in Galatians 3:10, 13, "But those who depend on the law to make them right with God are under his curse, for the Scriptures say, 'Cursed is everyone who does not observe and obey all the commands that are written in God's Book of the Law' [Deut. 27:26]. But Christ has rescued us from the curse pronounced by the law. When he was hung on the cross, he took upon himself the curse for our wrongdoing." There is nothing you can do on your own to save you from being cursed.

We know that no one is righteous, that we've all fallen short of the glory of God (Rom. 3:23). It's because we are under the curse of a fallen world. But hear the good news! "Yet God, in his grace, freely makes us right in his sight. He did this through Christ Jesus when he freed us from the penalty for our sins" (Rom. 3:24). Jesus took that curse on His shoulders when He died for you. He became a curse for you as He hung on that cross, so that you could be set free.

If you could describe the appearance of someone who is under a curse, you would probably picture them as downcast, despondent, disheartened, discouraged, dispirited, downhearted, sad, melancholy, gloomy, dismal, miserable, depressed, or dejected. And they live in fear.

Spiritual warfare is real. But God has given us a more than adequate defense in the form of our spiritual armor, described in Ephesians 6:10–17. We do not need additional procedures for dealing with "evil curses." We don't have to live in fear! When we confess our sins, repent of them and confess Jesus as our Lord, we enter into full and unrestricted freedom and blessing!

The Lord has told you what is good, and this is what he requires of you: to do what is right, to love mercy, and to walk humbly with your God.

— Micah 6:8

Obediently turning to God erases the curse and He blesses the home of the upright. In Part 2 tomorrow, we'll further discover the way we can stop the curse and achieve the blessed home.

TAKE ACTION

- Create a godly home by eliminating anything that could be construed as against God.
- Live your daily life as one who is freed from the curse. You are forgiven. Live that joy!

PRAY

Him:
- Thank God for giving you Jesus to remove the curse.
- Ask God to empower you with His whole armor.

Her:
- Thank God for setting you free from any discouragement in your life because you are fully forgiven.

ACHIEVING THE BLESSED HOME, Part 2

The L*ORD curses the house of the wicked, but he blesses the home of the upright.*

— Proverbs 3:33b

Throughout the Bible is a continual theme of "Blessings Follow Obedience." My wife and I mark verses in our Bibles that demonstrate this with "BFO." Today's Proverb is one of those verses. Do you want to live in a blessed home? A home that is full of joy, happiness, peacefulness and enjoyable? There are two steps in achieving this:

Obedience First

Obedience is faith in action. It demonstrates faith and produces faith. Obedience is pure loyalty to our Lord. It helps you focus on Him and what He has done for you. Obedience is not something you dread, or feel you should have to do. It is the joy of knowing your Lord and staying with Him so as to partake in His love and grow in Him further, deeper, and stronger. Obedience results in more maturity, becoming more usable to His glory, and becoming more expressible of His love to others.

Obedience is also the willingness to cooperate with God with His plans. It is lining up with His precepts and call. It is the self-surrender of your will so you'll become less and He becomes more. God delights in your obedience.

It is wrong to think, "When God blesses me, then I'll obey Him." That's backwards. That's pride and stubbornness. When we obey, He will not hold anything back.

For the Lord God is our sun and our shield. He gives us grace and glory. The Lord will withhold no good thing from those who do what is right.

— Psalm 84:11

Jesus replied, "But even more blessed are all who hear the word of God and put it into practice."

— Luke 11:28

Blessings Follow

Destruction will follow disobedience. There's also many verses about this. So you have a choice: obedience or disobedience—blessings or destruction.

So what exactly is a blessing? My dictionary states that it is God's favor and protection; something that brings well-being. To have God's hand of favor and protection on me motivates me to obey. I would like to challenge you to start a new way of greeting others. When someone asks, "How are you doing?" Respond with, "I am blessed." This mind-set reminds you God does have His hand on you, and what a beautiful way to start a conversation by revealing your blessings.*

A maximum marriage practices obedience in loyally serving God. Subsequently He promises blessings to their home *and* He delivers.

TAKE ACTION

- Discuss the armor of God in Ephesians 6:10–17 in living your daily lives in obedience.

PRAY

Him:
- Thank God for the joy of a blessed home.
- Ask God to empower you with His whole armor.

Her:
- Thank God for His many blessings in your marriage relationship.
- Ask God to give you a heart to live His Word and put it into practice.

---

*From *Minutes in His Presence, 52 Devotionals for Men* by Dennis R. Davidson, Copyright © 2018

CHARTING YOUR COURSE

The way of the godly leads to life; that path does not lead to death.
— Proverbs 12:28

It's a matter of life or death. Accepting Jesus as your Savior, and choosing to live a godly life, one where you're in right standing with God (having righteousness), brings a fuller life here, and also brings life eternal with Jesus. Death is not the end for the follower of Christ.

I choose life! I choose Jesus! Jesus said in John 10:10 that He came so you may have life, and that you may have it more abundantly. I believe He means here on Earth as well as in the hereafter. See how Solomon reiterates this in the following Proverb:

The path of life leads upward for the wise; they leave the grave behind.
— Proverbs 15:24

The book of Revelation portrays a beautiful picture of what it will be like where we'll spend all of eternity. "Then the angel showed me a river with the water of life, clear as crystal, flowing from the throne of God and of the Lamb. [2]It flowed down the center of the main street. On each side of the river grew a tree of life, bearing twelve crops of fruit, with a fresh crop each month. The leaves were used for medicine to heal the nations. [3]No longer will there be a curse upon anything. For the throne of God and of the Lamb will be there, and his servants will worship him"(Revelation 22:1–3).

That promise of life in the fullest sense should excite you to no end. It's all-inclusive. Jesus paid your way and everything is included for a comprehensive, lavish life. Determine the course you'll take.

The map to navigate life on earth has been provided to us through the Bible. Many search for happiness in "things" trying desperately to find the "happily ever after." Following the GPS of trusting God and His plan puts you on the right path towards a full life.

Nevertheless, many choose to follow their own GPS. They may

think it's the right way and possibly even the true way, because there are a lot of other people going that route, or a similar one. The world thinks that *any* road will take them to the "happily ever after."

There is a path before each person that seems right, but it ends in death.
— Proverbs 14:12 (See also Proverbs 16:25)

Jesus said, "I am the way, the truth, and the life" (John 14:6). *The* way. *The* truth. *The* life. There is no other way. The way of a maximum marriage stays on the course provided by Jesus. The Christian husband's and wife's feet are firmly planted on that path. They put Christ in the center of their decisions, their home-life, and their every circumstance. It's a vibrant marriage. It's an abundant marriage. It's a way of *life*!

Stay on the path that the Lord your God has commanded you to follow. Then you will live long and prosperous lives in the land you are about to enter and occupy.
— Deuteronomy 5:33

The path of the righteous is like the morning sun, shining ever brighter till the full light of day.
— Proverbs 4:18

TAKE ACTION

- Make the choice to follow the way of Jesus in all your decisions.

PRAY

Him: • Praise God for the full life He gives you here and eventually in Heaven.

Her: • Thank God for providing the map that shows how to navigate this life.

CHOOSING A HAPPY COUNTENANCE

A heart full of joy and goodness makes a cheerful face, But when a heart is full of sadness the spirit is crushed.
— Proverbs 15:13 (AMP)

When you're happy, it'll show by the sparkle in your eyes, your smile, and cheerful attitude. These attractive traits are cheap and easy to obtain — choose to be happy. When you are happy and excited, whether by circumstances or choice, you have extra energy, light, and life. This inner condition will give you a glow that is often contagious to those around you. A smile is always warm and inviting.

...For the happy heart, life is a continual feast.
— Proverbs 15:15b

The following acronym describes the secret to being full of joy.

J — Jesus first
O — Others second
Y — Yourself last

If you make a point to focus on Jesus — who is perfect, gracious, loving, and more — instead of your imperfections, or the imperfections of others, you can experience the true presence of the Holy Spirit. The reason that joy may be elusive is because you put yourself first and Jesus last. By abiding in Christ as a forgiven, reconciled, child of God you have everything you need to live in peace and joy.

Yet, even Solomon said in the third chapter of Ecclesiastes there is a time for sorrow — a time to cry and a time to grieve. You can see on someone's face when they have sorrow in their heart. Have you ever had someone ask you, when you're troubled or worried about something, "What's wrong?" It shows in your face. You can have experiences in your life that cause you to be broken-hearted. This scripture says that if you allow this sorrow to continue, it can break your spirit. A troubled heart clouds your face, as it saps your features and body of energy and vitality.

So, the key is to not dwell on painful circumstances. They will pass. God is in control. Choose to move on.

A smile is the best facial expression! A joyful soul enhances your appearance more than anything else. A happy face is a wonderful thing, and it is the result of a peaceful and contented heart. In your marriage, it will make living with each other more pleasant.

Every time you smile at someone, it is an action of love, a gift to that person, a beautiful thing.

— Mother Teresa

▩ TAKE ACTION

- Smile! Give away free smiles more often to your spouse. It'll brighten both of your faces.

▩ PRAY

Him:

- Thank God for being in control of your life and every circumstance you experience.
- Ask God to allow you to focus on having the joy of Jesus and spreading more smiles around to others.

Her:

- Ask God to keep you focused on having a happy heart.
- Thank God for your joy and ability to smile each day.

HAPPY LIFE, HEALTHY LIFE

A cheerful heart is good medicine, but a broken spirit saps a person's strength.

— Proverbs 17:22 (See also Proverbs 15:30)

Science has shown this Proverb to be true. Being happy helps promote a healthy lifestyle. Solomon was given this wisdom without all of the studies and research we've learned in recent years. Such as:

- Being happy may help keep your immune system strong, which might help you fight off the common cold and chest infections.
- Being happy reduces stress. Stress increases levels of the hormone cortisol, which can cause weight gain, disturbed sleep and high blood pressure. Happy people tend to produce lower levels of cortisol in response to stressful situations.
- Being happier can help lower blood pressure, which may decrease the risk of heart disease.
- Happier people live longer. This may be because they engage in more health-promoting behaviors, such as exercise.
- Being happy may reduce the perception of pain. It appears to be particularly effective in chronic pain conditions such as arthritis.

Being happy doesn't just make you feel better — it's also incredibly beneficial for your health. Here are six scientifically proven ways to become happier.

- **Express gratitude:** You can increase your happiness by focusing on the things you are grateful for. One way to practice gratitude is to write down three things you are grateful for at the end of each day.
- **Get active:** Aerobic exercise, also known as cardio, is the most effective type of exercise for increasing happiness. Walking or playing tennis won't just be good for your physical health, it'll help boost your mood too.
- **Get a good night's rest:** Lack of sleep can have a negative effect on your happiness. Learn to relax before going to bed. Create good bedroom habits for better sleep.

- **Spend time outside:** Go outside for a walk in the park, or get your hands dirty in the garden. It takes as little as five minutes of outdoor exercise to significantly improve your mood.
- **Eat a healthier diet:** Studies show that the more fruits and vegetables you eat, the happier you will be. What's more, eating more fruits and vegetables will also improve your health in the long-term.
- **Pray:** Regular time spent in prayer can increase happiness and also provide a host of other benefits, including reducing stress and improving sleep. Science has proven that people who pray tend to be statistically more healthy and live longer than those who do not.*

Being cheerful is a choice for a healthier life. A broken spirit does the opposite. Unhappy people have more health problems.

For a happier marriage, choose the happy, healthy lifestyle. The husband and wife who pursue happy habits together will reap the healthy benefits together.

TAKE ACTION

- Make a concentrated effort on making the proven ways mentioned above part of your daily routines.

PRAY

Him:
- Thank God for providing happiness in your life.
- Express gratitude for specific items He blessed you with today.
- Ask God for more chances to be more physically active in your lifestyle.

Her:
- Express gratitude towards God for your blessings.
- Ask God to give you good sleep.
- Thank God for beautiful days to spend outside.
- Thank God for your happiness.

*Source: healthline.com

LAUGHING FOR LONGEVITY

For the despondent, every day brings trouble; for the happy heart, life is a continual feast.

— Proverbs 15:15

Laughing is, and always will be, the best form of therapy. It crosses all communication barriers. Jesus says in John 10:10 that He came so that you may have life and have it more abundantly. If you are in Christ, you have a rich and satisfying life. Enjoy it! Have fun! Laugh!

I recommend having fun, because there is nothing better for people in this world than to eat, drink, and enjoy life. That way they will experience some happiness along with all the hard work God gives them.

— Ecclesiastes 8:15

Studies have actually shown that those couples who spend time laughing together were more likely to enjoy strong, positive relationships. The couple who laughs together stays together!

Other reports claim laughter reduces health problems, burns calories, and boosts blood flow. Science always backs up God's wisdom.

Occasionally life will bring heartache and you can easily become despondent. But don't stay in that environment. Count the blessings God has given you. Don't dwell on the difficulties. Discouragement will sink in. Look up! Remember Jesus has saved you, and through Him you have a rich life.

We were filled with laughter, and we sang for joy. And the other nations said, "What amazing things the Lord has done for them."

— Psalm 126:2

It isn't enough to just laugh in the presence of your spouse — it's the shared moments where you are both laughing together that really seem to count. There is one word from a movie my wife and I saw a long time ago that made us laugh hysterically when we heard it. To this day, when we repeat the word in the silly way it was said in the movie, it will still break us up.

Laughter makes for a continual feast. Who doesn't like a continual feast? It's utter enjoyment! Eat, drink and laugh! The apostle Paul tells us twice — no, three times (in Philippians 4:4 and 1 Thessalonians 5:16) — to rejoice always.

Be playful, give each other silly pet names, and create inside jokes that only you know about. Sharing a smile, a giggle, or even a guffaw with your spouse can break tension, create a sense of closeness, and improve communication. Keep in mind all the good you're doing the next time you break out into spontaneous laughter.

Enjoy life with your spouse, whom you love. Marriage is never meant to be drudgery.

There is nothing in the world so irresistibly contagious as laughter and good humor.

— Charles Dickens

TAKE ACTION

- Recall some moments in your lives that caused you to laugh. Initiate some new ways to create laughter and lightheartedness.

PRAY

Him:
- Thank God for laughter.
- Ask God to keep you from despondency and discouragement by keeping your focus on the blessings of life.

Her:
- Thank God for your husband's sense of humor.
- Thank God for Jesus who gives you life, and a life that is rich and satisfying.

TREADING THROUGH THE MISERY, Part 1

The human spirit can endure a sick body, but who can bear a crushed spirit?

— Proverbs 18:14

Discouragement and disappointment are common emotions as we face difficulties in life, and especially in married life. If you're not careful, depression and despondency may take over when circumstances don't go well. Solomon asks, "How do you overcome a broken spirit?"

He states we can endure through sickness, knowing that it can be a temporary thing. But when our spirit is crushed, it can be hard to overcome the gloom.

Remember first off that you are in good company. There are many characters in the Bible who faced discouragement. Among them were Job, Elijah, Jeremiah, Peter, and David (see his Psalms). But Solomon tells us what we need to do to fight discouragement in Proverbs 3:5–6, "Trust in the Lord with all your heart; do not depend on your own understanding. Seek His will in all you do, and He will show you which path to take."

Let's look at 5 steps to take when you're facing discouragement.* We'll study the first two today and the remaining three tomorrow.

1. Be honest. It's alright to express disappointment. It's alright to let others know you are discouraged. There is no need to hide it. But don't wallow in a self-pity party and don't bring others down with you. In Psalm 22, David expresses his discouragement starting with verse 1, "My God, my God, why have you abandoned me? Why are you so far away when I groan for help?" So first, be honest. Acknowledge your negative feelings, then you can have a target to shoot at in overcoming them. And pray, as David did, telling God of your disappointments. After the first 21 verses of Psalm 22, David turns his thoughts toward

God, getting his mind off of his own gloomy circumstances. Through the end of this Psalm, he proclaims His name, praising the Lord for all He has done. Then comes the powerful Psalm 23!

The Christian life is not a constant high. I have my moments of deep discouragement. I have to go to God in prayer with tears in my eyes, and say, "O God, forgive me," or "Help me."

— Billy Graham

2. Take care of yourself. Sometimes the circumstances of life drain us dry, and we need to pause, stop doing, and simply rest and refresh. When you're body is weak, then your thought processing can be weakened. Even through the discouragement, continue to eat and also exercise. Exercising is a good way to release the endorphins to make you feel better. Exercise has been shown to be both physically *and* mentally beneficial.

If there is a situation within your marriage that has you feeling down and discouraged, begin taking these steps to ease the pain of your crushed spirit.

The Lord is close to the brokenhearted and saves those who are crushed in spirit.

— Psalm 34:18 (NIV)

TAKE ACTION

- Read Psalm 23 out loud.

PRAY

Him: • Ask God for strength and endurance through the pain of discouragement. See Romans 12:12.

Her: • Go ahead and tell God about your disappointments. He's listening. See Psalm 34:18.

---

*Taken from "5 Ways to Stop Discouragement from Getting the Best of You" by Leslie Vernick, writer for The Association of Biblical Counselors (ABC). Copyright © 2019, Bible Study Tools.

TREADING THROUGH THE MISERY, Part 2

A joyful heart makes a cheerful face, But when the heart is sad, the spirit is broken.

— Proverbs 15:13 (NASB)

Continuing with our 5 steps to overcome discouragement, today we'll devote ourselves to steps 3 through 5.*

3. Think differently. As you grow in your spiritual walk, it's important to continually think on the positives of life. Philippians 4:8 says to fix your thoughts on what is true, honorable, right, pure, lovely, and admirable. And to think about things that are excellent and worthy of praise. Then God's peace will prevail.

Then Jesus said, "Come to me, all of you who are weary and carry heavy burdens, and I will give you rest."

— Matthew 11:28

4. Look for the eternal aspects. When the apostle Paul counsels to be transformed by the renewing of your mind (Romans 12:2), he is telling you that your mind needs to be trained to think differently (Step 3) than you have in the past. Learn to see both the temporal (life is hard) and the eternal (God has a purpose here) at the same time.

Paul speaks honestly of his temporal pain when he says he is hard pressed on every side, perplexed, persecuted and struck down. Yet he did not become crushed, despairing, abandoned, or destroyed. Why not? Because he learned to firmly fix the eternal perspective on his spiritual eyes. He says, "Therefore we do not lose heart.... So we fix our eyes not on what is seen, but on what is unseen. For what is seen is temporary, but what is unseen is eternal" (2 Corinthians 4:16, 18 NIV).

Paul never minimized the pain of the temporal, yet discouragement didn't win because he knew that God's purposes were at work. (See Philippians 1:12–14 for another example).

Rejoice in hope, be patient in tribulation, be constant in prayer.
— Romans 12:12 (ESV)

5. Draw near to God. The truth is life is hard, people will disappoint and hurt you, and you won't always understand God or His ways. But if you're not in a close trusting relationship with God, life's troubles can become unbearable. Keep on praying. Keep on reading His Word. Keep enduring. Look at what you'll reap:

Let's not get tired of doing what is good. At just the right time we will reap a harvest of blessing if we don't give up.
— Galatians 6:9

If you find yourself in a discouraging time in your marriage, gratitude is a powerful anecdote. You may find it hard to give God thanks for the difficult situation that you're in, but you can learn to look for things to be thankful for in the midst of it. Being thankful for what you have can make your heart joyful, thereby destroying the sadness of the broken spirit. "The Lord is my shepherd; I have all that I need" (Psalm 23:1).

TAKE ACTION

- Here are some verses to read when you are discouraged: Joshua 1:9; Psalm 27:14; Isaiah 41:10; John 14:27; John 16:33; Hebrews 4:16; Philippians 4:17; 1 Peter 1:6–9.

PRAY

Him: • Ask God to open your eyes to the good in your life and close your eyes to the negatives.

Her: • Ask God to give you perseverance through the difficult times.

---

*Taken from "5 Ways to Stop Discouragement from Getting the Best of You" by Leslie Vernick, writer for The Association of Biblical Counselors (ABC). Copyright © 2019, Bible Study Tools.

CONFIDENTLY CLIMBING OUT OF THE PIT

Worry weighs a person down; an encouraging word cheers a person up.
— Proverbs 12:25

We reviewed this Proverb — concentrating on the second half — in the devotional entitled Complimenting and Praising (page 58). Now let's focus on the first part.

Worrying and being anxious proclaims you're not confident God knows what He is doing. Ouch! That's a punch in my gut. That tells me how weak my faith is. Isaiah 55:8–9 says, "'For my thoughts are not your thoughts, neither are your ways my ways,' declares the Lord. 'As the heavens are higher than the earth, so are my ways higher than your ways and my thoughts than your thoughts.'" Repeat to yourself, "Since God is in control, I can be confident His ways are best."

Now faith is confidence in what we hope for and assurance about what we do not see.
— Hebrews 11:1 (NIV)

Allowing discouragement to conquer your thoughts will only bring on worry which will weigh you down deeper into the pit of disappointment. Yes, life can get you down. Yes, people will let you down. Yes, your spouse will disappoint you at some time. Don't be discouraged. Let it go and visually hand over your situation to God. Rest in Him. And then go about your day in confidence.

Rejoice in our confident hope. Be patient in trouble, and keep on praying.
— Romans 12:12

Be confident, patient, and pray. Good all-around advice from Paul. Be willing to listen to God. Don't try to drown out His voice to pursue your own way. Sometimes disappointments happen because you fail to trust in His timing. Just because God doesn't do something today doesn't mean that He is not going to do it tomorrow. Always remember this: God sees what you can't see and He knows what you don't know. Trusting in His timing is crucial. His timing is always right on time! Proverbs 20:24 says, "The LORD directs our steps."

Now I believe there is another way to confidently climb out of the pit of discouragement, and Solomon reveals it in the second part of today's Proverb. Certainly, when you're feeling down, an encouraging word from another will cheer you up. But you can't expect an encourager to always be around when you need one.

Notice that Solomon doesn't say which person will be cheered up. The encourager can be the one who gets cheered up as well. Psychologists will tell you the best way to get over depression or disappointment is to do something kind for another person, like giving them a compliment. When you're feeling down, it can be really hard to initiate a compliment towards someone else, especially if you're the one needing the encouraging word. But do it. Blessing others will bless you.

The best way to cheer yourself is to try to cheer someone else up.
— Mark Twain

A maximum marriage overcomes discouragement by being confident that God is in control of everything. In marriage, patience must be cultivated while you wait for God's perfect timing to work things out.

TAKE ACTION

- Discuss with each other how you need to lean on each other when life gets you down and how encouragement is needed.

PRAY

Him: • Thank God for being in control of your life.

Her: • Pour out to God your disappointments and then thank Him for working out the solutions.

REGULATING THE TEMPERATURE

A hot-tempered person starts fights; a cool-tempered person stops them.
— Proverbs 15:18

If you're human, you have probably experienced some form of anger towards someone or some thing in the past week. Or yesterday. Or even today. Especially if you're married, this emotional agitation can flair up many times. It is a God-given emotion. Everyone has the ability to express anger of some kind (see also page 128).

Anger in and of itself is not necessarily a bad thing. Paul says in the very first part of Ephesians 4:26 to be angry. You can be angry for a cause. It is okay to feel passionate about something. But not to the degree that it destroys. You don't need to impose your will on others with rage. Paul immediately goes on to state, "and do not sin." If you allow anger to change your demeanor for the worse, you are not letting the Holy Spirit control you.

Don't sin by letting anger control you.
— Psalm 4:4

An angry person starts fights; a hot-tempered person commits all kinds of sin.
— Proverbs 29:22

Anger has many degrees of heat. It can be a simmering, mild irritation or it can be a blazing hot explosion. Someone who has a loss of self-control is described as quick-tempered or hot-tempered. A slow-tempered or cool-tempered person is calm, collected and mild.

A soft answer turns away wrath, but a harsh word stirs up anger.
— Proverbs 15:1 (ESV)

When a situation gets heated and it starts to get hot, an uncontrolled thermostat will do great damage. Calming down and controlling the heat slowly is a mark of strength. Turn down the heat and be cool!

Whoever restrains his words has knowledge, and he who has a cool spirit is a man of understanding.
— Proverbs 17:27 (ESV)

A firefighter knows the danger of letting a fire get out of control. They know to respond quickly. You can always feel it when anger is starting to boil up within you. When anger starts to rage out of control and consume you, don't fan the flames. Respond methodically by turning it over to God.

A quarrelsome person starts fights as easily as hot embers light charcoal or fire lights wood.
— Proverbs 26:21

To maximize your marriage relationship, make a point to be cool. Allow the Holy Spirit to calmly control you. If you are on the receiving end of someone who is being harsh and angry, be cool and speak softly. If you notice you're the angry one, take a time-out and cool down before you say or do something you'll regret. Controlled cooling is a powerful force that can unleash godly love towards each other.

TAKE ACTION

- Talk about things that make each of you angry. Are they good causes? Are they trivial things? Ask each other for help in the areas that can cause anger to flair up. See Proverbs 20:3.

PRAY

Him: • Ask God to teach you how to be cool in the midst of strife.

Her: • Ask God to give you a sense of calmness and peacefulness in controlling conflict and things that stir up anger.

SLOWING DOWN TO SHOW LOVE

Good sense makes one slow to anger; and it is his glory to overlook an offense.

— Proverbs 19:11

A controlled person will not let something that someone said or did make them agitated or irritated. It makes good sense to be calmly in control. Having good sense will slow you down so that you don't overreact and jump to wrong conclusions.

Love is slow to anger (1 Cor. 13:5). I think that is worth repeating — *love is slow to anger*. Being able to slow down eruptions of anger is a way to express love. Galatians 5:22 says the Holy Spirit produces this kind of fruit in our lives: love, joy, peace, patience, kindness, goodness, faithfulness, gentleness, and self-control. You can't have any of these attributes if anger is controlling you. Being slow to anger is a characteristic of God.

...Be slow to anger, for the anger of man does not produce the righteousness of God.

— James 1:19b–20 (ESV)

The Lord is merciful and gracious, slow to anger and abounding in steadfast love.

— Psalm 103:8 (ESV) (See also Psalm 145:8 and Nahum 1:3)

Notice that scripture doesn't say God is never angry. His anger is slow to erupt because of His vast love for you. He is not quick-tempered. If you identify with being quick-tempered, remember that love covers all wrongs (Prov. 10:12). Just as the Lord is merciful and gracious to you, you should be to others as well (Eph. 4:31).

It is much wiser to trust God with your spouse, instead of trying to correct them with your anger (which is the wrong approach altogether). God's discipline is much more thorough and precise. Loving God means trusting Him. Loving your spouse means adjusting for the little things that really don't matter. Is it really worth it to get all worked up if your wife takes a long time to get ready to go somewhere? Is it really worthwhile to angrily complain about the husband who doesn't get things done on your time table? Adjust! Let it go and move on (see page 128 on the differences between love and anger).

But love *can* be angry. You should be angry about abuse of drugs or alcohol. You should be angry if your spouse is controlled by sin. Being slow to anger doesn't turn its head to wrongs, but love rises above and offers compassion. Being slow to anger and demonstrating tough love means you are concerned and want the best for the other. Love unconditionally instead of trying to intimidate through anger. Love more and be angry less. Above all else, be rich in love and slow to anger (Psalm 145:8). That makes good sense!

Whoever is slow to anger has great understanding, but he who has a hasty temper exalts folly.

— Proverbs 14:29 (ESV)

TAKE ACTION

- Ask forgiveness, if necessary, if your frustrations took control of you over something your spouse did or said.
- When you feel anger coming on, do these 2 things to slow down:
  1. Breathe. Take a deep breath, relax and calm down.
  2. Pray together. Ask the other to allow the Spirit to take over and control the situation before anger causes any damage.

PRAY

Him: • Ask God to teach you how to be slow to anger.

Her: • Thank God for his mercies, grace and steadfast love.

CONQUERING THE FURY

Fools vent their anger, but the wise quietly hold it back.
— Proverbs 29:11

In order to conquer this enemy called anger, it is necessary to understand it. Where does it come from? Why am I attacking? What am I defending? There are four underlying sources that anger springs from.

1. Hurt. If you have been wounded in your past and are scarred from rejection or emotional pain of some kind, anger can be a protective wall that keeps people at bay and pain away. You don't want to be hurt again, so you lash out to protect yourself.

2. Injustice. When you feel like you have been violated of what you perceive to be wrong, unfair and unjust, anger may be triggered. This is especially true when someone who is close to you and whom you love has treated you unjustly.

3. Fear. We all need to feel secure. When you feel threatened, you may get angry because you are afraid of the changing circumstances. Ask yourself, "What am I afraid of?" Put your faith in God over your fear.

4. Frustration. Unmet expectations, either in yourself or another, can lead to anger. People will always let you down. You'll let yourself down. Being frustrated from the let-downs can result in anger.

Be not quick in your spirit to become angry, for anger lodges in the heart of fools.
— Ecclesiastes 7:9 (ESV)

Anger can also be used as a manipulative tactic to get your inner needs met. Whether it's to address your inner hurts, inner fears, or frustrations, you want to be loved and feel significant. Security should not be built on others, but only in Christ (Phil. 4:19).

To conquer anger, consider taking these steps to alter your attitude, as outlined in Philippians 2:2–8:

— Have the goal to be like-minded with Christ.

— Give the other person preferential treatment.
— Consider the other person's interests.
— Do not emphasize your position or rights.
— Look for ways to demonstrate a servant's heart.
— Speak and act with a humble spirit.
— Be willing to die to your own desires (Don't be selfish).*

Avoiding a fight is a mark of honor; only fools insist on quarreling.
— Proverbs 20:3

Be smart. Take control of your anger. Demonstrate the grace of God by establishing the following to yourself: "I have placed my anger on the cross with Christ. I will no longer be controlled by anger." And declare Ephesians 4:30–31 as your charge: "Get rid of all bitterness, rage, anger, harsh words, and slander, as well as all types of evil behavior. Instead, be kind to each other, tenderhearted, forgiving one another, just as God through Christ has forgiven you." A marriage relationship will flourish with these two verses as the foundation.

TAKE ACTION

- If you are still battling anger's control, seek a professional Christian counselor to help you. Don't think of getting counseling as a sign of weakness. It's a sign of strength.
- Concentrate each day on one of the seven steps mentioned from Philippians 2:2–8. In one week you should be well on your way in overcoming anger.

PRAY

Him: • Ask God to help you conquer the strains of anger's control.

Her: • Ask God to give you the mind of Christ at all times.

*Taken from *Counseling Through Your Bible Handbook*. Copyright © 2008 by June Hunt. Hope for the Heart, Inc. Published by Harvest House Publishers. Eugene, OR 97408

RECOGNIZING THE HIDDEN DANGER

Wrath is cruel, anger is overwhelming…

— Proverbs 27:4 (ESV)

"The idea that a Christian is never allowed to be angry is a demonic myth that tends to produce neurotic anxiety," says RC Sproil. "Anger is not in itself sinful, but...it may be the occasion for sin. The issue of self-control is the question of how we deal with anger. **Violence, tantrums, bitterness, resentment, hostility, and even withdrawn silence are all sinful responses to anger.**"

Control of anger is the key. Solomon has warned in a multitude of Proverbs the danger of anger because of its hidden vices. If you don't control anger, it will most certainly overwhelm you with sinful responses. Proverbs 10:11 says, "The mouth of the wicked conceals violence." And Proverbs 16:29 states, "A man of violence entices his neighbor in a way that is not good" (ESV).

Left unchecked, anger destroys you.

Anger is an acid that can do more harm to the vessel in which it is stored than to anything on which it is poured.

— Mark Twain

A man without self-control is like a city broken into and left without walls.

— Proverbs 25:28 (ESV)

Left unchecked, anger can build resentment. See how Charles Swindoll puts it:

> "Allowed to fester through neglect, the toxic fumes of hatred foam to a boil within the steamroom of the soul. Pressure mounts to a maddening magnitude. By then it's only a matter of time. The damage is always tragic, often irreparable: a battered child; a crime of passion; ugly, caustic words; loss of a job; a runaway; a bad record; domestic disharmony; or

a ruined testimony. None of this is new. Solomon described the problem long ago:

> 'Pretty words may hide a wicked heart, just as a pretty glaze covers a common clay pot. A man with hate in his heart may sound pleasant enough, but don't believe him; for he is cursing you in his heart. Though he pretends to be so kind, his hatred will finally come to light for all to see' (Proverbs 26:23–26, TLB).

> "The answer to resentment isn't complicated, it's just painful. It requires *honesty*. You must first admit it's there. It then requires *humility*. You must confess it before the One who died for such sins. It may even be necessary for you to make it right with those you have offended out of resentful bitterness. Finally, it requires *vulnerability*—a willingness to keep that tendency submissive to God's regular reproof, and a genuinely teachable, unguarded attitude."*

Recognize that any one of these hidden dangers that spring from unchecked anger will destroy a marriage. A strong marriage will make amends to destroy those vices. How? Either by willful counseling, prayer, or kindness. The power couple is deliberate about shattering those sins from unmanaged anger through the power of Jesus Christ.

TAKE ACTION

- Anger can cause you to fight or run. Neither of those resolve anything. Talk about which of anger's vices you struggle with. Be honest, humble and vulnerable. Proceed to pray for each other about them.

PRAY

Him:
- Ask God to empower your wife with the ability to overcome anger's hidden dangers.
- Thank God for His forgiveness when you have fallen short.

Her:
- Ask God to rebuke Satan's hold on any of your husband's anger issues.

*Taken from *Growing Strong in the Seasons of Life* by Charles R. Swindoll. Copyright © 1983, 1994, 2007 by Charles R. Swindoll, Inc. Zondervan Publishing.

CONFIDENTLY BEING SAFE AND STILL, Part 1

The name of the LORD *is a strong fortress; the godly run to him and are safe.*

— Proverbs 18:10

Solomon knew that the Lord was the One in whom he could find safety and security — not his own wealth, wisdom or splendor. Perhaps he learned this from his own father. Look what David had to say:

The LORD *is my rock and my fortress and my deliverer, my God, my rock, in whom I take refuge, my shield, and the horn of my salvation, my stronghold.*

— Psalm 18:2 (ESV)

David also refers to the Lord as a place of safety in Psalm 46. Martin Luther used this Psalm for his inspiration in writing the old hymn, "A Mighty Fortress Is Our God." It portrays the hope you can have during the struggles of life. When life's storms come (and they will), you can find refuge in the mighty fortress of our God.

A mighty fortress is our God,
a bulwark never failing;
our helper He, amid the flood
of mortal ills prevailing.
For still our ancient foe
does seek to work us woe;
his craft and power are great,
and armed with cruel hate,
on earth is not his equal.

This hymn is a celebration of the sovereign power of God over all earthly and spiritual forces, and of the confident hope we have in Him because of Christ. It shows how you can be assured in tough and difficult times. In any time of need, when you battle with the forces of evil, God is your fortress to hide in and protect you, and the Word that endures forever will fight for you.

I picture an infant peacefully sleeping in the arms of its mother or father. Is there anything more beautifully calming and soothing than that image? There is value in just being still. Psalm 46:10 says, "Be still, and know that I am God!" It expresses the idea of confidently leaving everything in the hands of God.

A husband and wife who take refuge in the Lord, abiding in Him through any situation, are safe. "If God is for us, who can ever be against us?" (Rom. 8:31) God is in control even in your dark times. Hang on, don't ever give up. Place yourself in His arms, be still, and rest peacefully, trusting that He will fight your battles for you.

> My hope is built on nothing less
> Than Jesus' blood and righteousness;
> I dare not trust the sweetest frame,
> But wholly lean on Jesus' name.
> On Christ, the solid Rock, I stand;
> All other ground is sinking sand,
> All other ground is sinking sand.*

TAKE ACTION

- Read Psalm 46.
- Make an appointed time to be still, away from the demands of the day, and observe the beauty of what God has given you and stand in awe of His power.

PRAY

Him: • Praise God for being your strong fortress and safe place.

Her: • Praise God for giving you security when the difficulties of life overwhelm you. Give them to Him now if you are experiencing them.

---

* "The Solid Rock" by Edward Mote, 1797–1874

CONFIDENTLY BEING SAFE AND STILL, Part 2

Whoever fears the Lord has a secure fortress, and for their children it will be a refuge.

— Proverbs 14:26 (NIV)

The maximum marriage home is one centered around the Lord. Their home is a secure castle because they have a personal awareness of the awesome and majestic sovereignty of God. I believe that environment can best be done in stillness.

If you have children, you know it can become chaotic within the home. Whatever age they are, there is always something going on. It can be hard for children to be still. If there is constant noise, such as crying, or the TV blasting away, there is no peace. A lack of quietness imparts a lack of safety. No one can feel secure in mayhem. It is disorder and generates complication.

On the other hand, when there is a discipline of being still and quiet, there can be a strong sense of security. Learn to press the pause button. Create a household that portrays a safe place of peacefulness. This honors God.

In the rush and noise of life, as you have intervals, step home within yourselves and be still. Wait upon God, and feel His good presence; this will carry you evenly through your day's business.

— William Penn

How can this "stillness" be accomplished? First, a family that prays together stays together. Praying is a peaceful practice. Second, a family that reads the Bible together quietly listens to God speaking. The quieter you become, the more you can hear. A home where there is prayer and listening to God gives a sense of shelter and protection from the world's ambushing.

When a family member is experiencing a struggle or difficulty, how reassuring it is to have a home they can run to for safety. How reassuring for a husband to come home to his wife after an extremely difficult day at work, knowing his wife will comfort him by praying with him and for him. When a wife has had everything go wrong in her day, how comforting to know that her husband will give her insecurities over to the Lord through prayer and lift her spirits with godly wisdom. How comforting for children to know their parents are stable, steady in godliness, and will encourage them through all their problems.

The LORD *will fight for you; you need only to be still.*
— Exodus 14:14

Standing still in awe of the great Creator is a home security system that protects the home like no other. A God-centered marriage *is* a secure fortress.

You will be secure, because there is hope; you will look about you and take your rest in safety.
— Job 11:18 (NIV)

TAKE ACTION

- Create the environment within your home as one of quietness and stillness. Watch how it becomes secure, safe, and stable.
- If there was anyone who felt an uneasiness and lack of stability, it could have been Job. Reflect on Job 11:18.

PRAY

Him:
- Ask God help you to confidently create a home environment of peacefulness.
- Thank God for your secure home fortress.

Her:
- Ask God to fill your home with His Spirit.
- Thank God for allowing you to raise your children to be stable.

SATURATING IN TRANQUILITY

Whoever listens to me will live in safety and be at ease, without fear of harm.

— Proverbs 1:33 (NIV)

"Houston, Tranquility Base here. The Eagle has landed." With those words, NASA astronaut Neil Armstrong reported back to Earth that the long, hard mission of landing a man on the moon had finally been accomplished. What a brilliant idea to call their landing site Tranquility Base. They had landed in the southwestern corner of the lunar lava-plain called Mare Tranquillitatis ("Sea of Tranquility"). Tranquility means peacefulness, calmness, quietness, or stillness.

Can you describe your life as one being in a sea of tranquility or as one being in a sea of turmoil? Seeking God's wisdom will allow you to live in tranquility (in safety and at ease). Today's Proverb is the last verse in the first chapter on how God's wisdom is to be continually sought after for a life of peace, untroubled by fear of harm.

If turmoil has you surrounded, and that's all you can see, rest in the assurance that God has you in His everlasting arms.

The eternal God is your refuge, and his everlasting arms are under you. He drives out the enemy before you; he cries out, "Destroy them!"

— Deuteronomy 33:27

This verse from Deuteronomy was the inspiration behind the words of the hymn, "Leaning On The Everlasting Arms" by Elisha A. Hoffman. Shortened, her words were:

What a fellowship, what a joy divine,
What a blessedness, what a peace is mine,
Leaning on the everlasting arms.

O how sweet to walk in this pilgrim way,
O how bright the path grows from day to day,
Leaning on the everlasting arms.

What have I to dread, what have I to fear,
I have blessed peace with my Lord so near,
Leaning on the everlasting arms.

Safe and secure from all alarms;
Leaning, leaning, leaning on the everlasting arms.

If you love and pursue God's wisdom, He will comfort you with tranquility. The choice is yours. Peace and safety. Or fear and destruction. What a difference! God offers you the secure life. Peace and protection make a strong tranquility base — they can be yours by leaning on His everlasting arms.

*It took a special act of creation to bring [rest] into being, that the universe would be incomplete without it. What was created on the seventh day? Tranquility, serenity, peace and repose.**
— Abraham Joshua Hershcel

Tough times? God is your refuge. Rest. Be still. Breathe. Make the choice to live in the sea of tranquility for your marriage. God destroys your enemies of distress and uneasiness. That's great comfort to saturate yourself in.

TAKE ACTION

- Make your home a Sea of Tranquility — peacefulness, calmness, quietness, or stillness.

PRAY

Him:
- Thank God for His everlasting arms that uphold you.
- Praise God for being able to walk through trials in peace.

Her:
- Thank God for destroying the things that would keep you from the tranquil life He wants for you.
- Thank God for safety and security from all distress.

* *The Sabbath: Its Meaning for Modern Man* by Abraham Joshua Herschel Copyright © 2005. (First published in 1951) Farrar Straus & Giroux

VALUING YOUR ROLES

Who can find a virtuous and capable wife? She is more precious than rubies.

— Proverbs 31:10

Much has been written on the woman of Proverbs 31. For this study, I wish to emphasize the husband-wife relationship of Proverbs 31. The woman of Proverbs 31 is certainly one of noble character, but the man in her life is just as valuable in their home-building.

Verses 10–31 are written in the form of an acrostic poem with each successive verse beginning with one of the 22 letters in the Hebrew alphabet. This communicates a sense of totality, and of outlining the woman's virtues. These traits include hardworking, generous, passionate, caring, industrious, a sacrificial heart, a good speaker, loves to laugh, and she enjoys her family. The virtuous woman is meant to show the expression of Proverb's continual theme of wisdom and celebrating her everyday roles. She desires to be a godly woman—a woman led by the wisdom of God.

However, the core of these verses is directed at the supporting role of the man. They are not commands to women, but a recognition of how men should appreciate the woman's role and accomplishments. The overall theme is concluded in the last verse which declares the man to "honor her for all that her hands have done."

By no means should a husband hold these verses up as a standard ideal. No woman is capable of living up to this "perfection." "Who can find a virtuous wife?" is a rhetorical question for the man to understand the valuable treasure — the rare jewel — that God has given him specifically.

The word "virtuous" is the Hebrew word "valor" meaning "strength, might, efficiency, wealth, army." Valor isn't about what the woman does, but how she does it. If you are a stay-at-home mom, be a stay-at-home mom of valor. If you are a nurse, be a nurse of valor. If you are a CEO, a waitress, rich or poor—do it all with valor. You are a warrior!

And the man is to cheer her valor with encouragement. He is to celebrate all of her accomplishments, large and small. See how verse 28 says "the husband praises her"and then again in verse 30, "she will be greatly praised."

Proverbs 31:10–31 is a superior model for a maximum marriage. Love excels because of this couple's earnest commitment to God and to each other. They glorify God in all they do. Others around them can't help but notice, and their relationship stands the test of time.

TAKE ACTION

- Make a commitment to become a Proverbs 31 couple by supporting each other's roles and complimenting each other's accomplishments. Praise each other specifically for something the other has blessed you with this week.

PRAY

Him:
- Praise God for particular accomplishments your wife does around the home.
- Ask God to give you a new sense of appreciation for your wife's value.

Her:
- Ask God to make you a woman of valor in all that you do.
- Ask God for forgiveness if you have complained about your job outside the home or inside the home.

HARMONIOUS COMPANIONS

Her husband can trust her, and she will greatly enrich his life.
— Proverbs 31:11

A maximum, virtuous marriage has two team members that work together in harmony. They are a team where chemistry is demonstrated between both of them, and they work at keeping that chemistry. There is complete trust in each other. No controlling. No manipulation. Only trust.

When you trust your spouse, you allow them to prosper in everything they do. The trusting husband who builds up his wife allows her to grow and blossom into a beautiful, successful woman. The trusting wife allows her husband to be a strong leader and gives him confidence in everything he does. They thrive off each other's trust.

Trust is built over time and must be maintained, and it can be destroyed in an instant. Yet it can always be restored. Honesty in your relationship is so important. You can't build a strong marriage on half-truth and half-lies. You must be honest at all times.

How do you build trust? John Gottman says, "Trust is built in very small moments in which one person turns toward their partner when they're in need. When our partner responds positively, by 'being there' for us, that builds trust."

Do you respond positively to some of the "biggies" in marriage — communication, money, children, sex, and in-laws? A good team will collaborate for the sake of unity. You won't agree on everything, but working on a compromise can be essential for strengthening the bond between each other.

Husbands and wives are to be on the same level. Many a husband has believed in order to be the leader, he must rule over the home. There is a difference between being in authority and being an authoritarian. An authoritarian shows a lack of concern for the wishes or opinions of others, is domineering, and dictatorial. No one likes to be under that type of person. And the authoritarian will never be satisfied himself. Being a confident person of authority encourages and builds up the other team member. And thus brings more satisfaction.

Now the wife must be trustworthy. She must prove herself capable of her husband's confidence in her.

A worthy wife is a crown for her husband, but a disgraceful woman is like cancer in his bones.

— Proverbs 12:4

Solomon says then the husband is to trust his wife. He doesn't have to constantly try to manipulate or belittle her. In this complete trust, his wife can shine and greatly enrich his life.

It works both ways. The husband must be trustworthy. A wife who completely trusts her husband will be enriched by him.

Don't take each other for granted. Remember every day what is really important in your life. Give your spouse reasons to have confidence in you. The trust, love and respect will grow under this nurturing. The marriage becomes a symphony in harmony.

Love bears all things, believes all things, hopes all things, endures all things.

— 1 Corinthians 13:7 (ESV)

TAKE ACTION

- Build each other up with words of affirmation and admiration.

PRAY

Him:

- Ask God to make you a trustworthy husband.
- Ask God to make you a leader, but not an authoritarian.
- Thank God for the longevity of your marriage.

Her:

- Ask God to make you a trustworthy wife.
- Thank God for your enriched lives through trust.

BRINGING GOOD TO EACH OTHER

She brings him good, not harm, all the days of her life.
— Proverbs 31:12

The wife's lifestyle is to portray a dislike of ungodliness and worldly desires. She lives sensibly, righteously, and godly because her time is full of being zealous for good deeds. Her enthusiasm excels in showering her husband with good qualities.

A wife sharing goodness brings good to the family, and thereby, goodness is returned back to her. First Timothy 3:11 says, "Wives must be respected and must not slander others. They must exercise self-control and be faithful in everything they do." A supporting, faithful wife enables her husband to serve in the high calling of deacon. And in return, he must be faithful to her and manage his household well. A deacon will be rewarded with respect from others and will have increased confidence in their faith in Christ Jesus (1 Timothy 3:13). It's all traced back to his wife. It is no wonder the old saying is true: "Behind every successful man is a woman."

What are some "good" qualities a wife can bring to her husband? She...

- Is pleasant to be around;
- Does not nag;
- Allows him his space;
- Shows confidence in working out problems;
- Has a great sense of humor;
- Takes good care of the house;
- Always looks good for him;
- Encourages him;
- Supports him;
- Seeks to always be growing spiritually.

Subsequently, the husband is to bring good to his wife. He...

- Is trustworthy;
- Shows sincerity in loving her;

- Is responsible;
- Works hard at his job;
- Is honest;
- Listens well and attentively;
- Shows sensitivity;
- Has a great sense of humor;
- Works at communicating effectively;
- Seeks to always be growing spiritually.

Don't miss the two little words in the middle of today's verse: *not harm*. Satan will make it easy for you to hurt the one closest to you. Be careful not to disrespect, nag, be selfish, or criticize harshly.

The husband and wife team concentrating on sharing good qualities all the days of their lives will have a maximum marriage.

Get rid of all bitterness, rage, anger, harsh words, and slander, as well as all types of evil behavior. Instead, be kind to each other, tenderhearted, forgiving one another, just as God through Christ has forgiven you.
— Ephesians 4:31–32

Fix your thoughts on what is true, and honorable, and right, and pure, and lovely, and admirable. Think about things that are excellent and worthy of praise.
— Philippians 4:8

TAKE ACTION

- Take an honest assessment of your personal good qualities and ask the other for support in those areas which are lacking.

PRAY

Him:
- Thank God for the goodness your wife brings to your life.
- Ask God to help you excel in goodness back to her.

Her:
- Ask God to consume you with good qualities everyday towards your husband.
- Thank God for His goodness.

SERVING OTHERS TOGETHER

[23]Her husband is well known at the city gates, where he sits with the other civic leaders. [26]When she speaks, her words are wise, and she gives instructions with kindness.

— Proverbs 31:23; 26

Here is a picture of a thriving, maximum marriage. Both the husband and the wife are mentors. They have gotten their personal relationship in order and have a passionate desire to help others.

This husband is honored and respected in the community where he lives. Taking a seat with the elders at the city gates was a great honor because it was where all public business occurred and was similar to the city's courtroom. He was counseling others and judging disputes and such. In order to gain this respect, a man would have to be well-dressed, clean, and have his family life in order. Part of having his family life in order would mean having a good wife because she would make sure her husband was neat in appearance, dressed in the finest clothing they could afford, and work hard herself so that her husband would have time to participate in these community events.

As you read through the attributes of a virtuous woman in Proverbs 31, verse 23 seems to be out of place. But part of being a virtuous wife is respecting her husband. If she doesn't respect him, others will not respect him. One could tell if a man had a good wife because of his cheerful manner and pleasant humor. I think that all boils down to the fact that a man with a good wife is a happy man. Simplistically, the truism "happy wife, happy life" is biblical!

While it is stated that the husband is a counselor of wise advice, the wife is also (v.26). Together, they reflect the same image of couples that Paul tells Titus about in Titus 2:1–5. He says the older men were to exercise self-control, to be worthy of respect, and to live wisely. They were to have sound faith and be filled with love and patience.

Similarly, the older women were to live in a way that honors God. They were not to slander others or to be heavy drinkers. Instead, they should teach others what is good. These older women were to train the younger women to love their husbands and their children, to live wisely and to be pure, to work in their homes, to do good, and to be submissive to their own husbands. Then, they would not bring shame on the word of God. In this way, they would make the teaching about God our Savior attractive in every way (Titus 2:10).

The Titus 2 couple and the Proverbs 31 couple are the same — living godly lives and serving others with godly advice. Don't think this is just for elderly couples because of the description of older men and older women. In her book, *Adorned*, Nancy DeMoss Wolgemuth says, "Whether you're young and aging or not so young and aging, you can be a vibrant, thriving, fruitful model for as long as God gives you breath."*

And the result? By blessing others with your gained wisdom in life, you will be blessed. You are made by God to serve others. A "maximum marriage" couple mentors together.

We should help others do what is right and build them up in the Lord. For even Christ didn't live to please himself.

— Romans 15:2, 3b

TAKE ACTION

- Seek out ways you can help others by mentoring. Don't think you're not qualified. You are filled with the Holy Spirit who will give you power beyond your abilities.

PRAY

Him:
- Thank God for the respect your wife gives to you.
- Ask God to give you wisdom to help others.

Her:
- Ask God to fill you with respectfulness towards your husband.
- Ask God to give you the motivation and courage to help others.

**Adorned, Living Out the Beauty of the Gospel Together*, p.64, © 2017 Nancy DeMoss Wolgemuth. Moody Publishers, Chicago, IL 60610

PRAISING EACH OTHER

28Her children stand and bless her. Her husband praises her: 29"There
are many virtuous and capable women in the world, but you surpass
them all!" 30Charm is deceptive, and beauty does not last; but a wom-
an who fears the LORD *will be greatly praised. 31Reward her for all*
she has done. Let her deeds publicly declare her praise.

— Proverbs 31:28–31

These verses are loaded with the importance of complimentary words! (See also page 58 on Complimenting and Praising)

This is a home where commendations abound. There are no insults or put-downs. It's quite different than what you see on television sit-coms, don't you think? Characters on sit-coms try to get in the best cheap-shot for a laugh or for a feeling of superiority.

Solomon states a maximum home life exhibits the opposite. In a home where children see their parents faithfully serving God, persevering through trials, and seeing integrity demonstrated, allows them to feel a sense of security and confidence in their own lives. I believe in this virtuous home the parents are praising the children in everything they do. The parents are looking for the positive traits in their child and not concentrating on the negative. Webster's dictionary defines a blessing as "a thing conducive to happiness or welfare." When the child is blessed, the parents are blessed, creating a happy home.

In verse 29, the father of this household showers the mother with the compliment of all compliments: "You are the best in the world!" In verse 30, she is described as a godly woman, one who fears the Lord (see page 10 on Fearing God for Wisdom). Such a woman is to be greatly praised. Such a man should be greatly praised as well. The communication within this marriage is bubbling over with building up and stimulating each other.

Encourage each other and build each other up....

— 1 Thessalonians 4:11

...Let everything you say be good and helpful, so that your words will be an encouragement to those who hear them.

— Ephesians 4:29

Now, after most of this chapter has shown what a virtuous wife is, she is to be rewarded, and her accomplishments make her a positive public example. The New King James Version states that "her own works praise her in the gates." Remember back in verse 23, the husband is known in the gates and is honored throughout the community. He does not stifle or restrict the honor his wife is to receive, even if it might match or exceed his own. A husband's rewarding of his wife encourages her spirit and provides for further productivity.

This virtuous, maximum marriage blooms because of praise all around! The Lord praises a godly marriage when they do well, and their accomplishments will be rewarded. "Be diligent so that you receive your full reward" (2 John 1:8). Always make the effort to build up your marriage. As Psalm 37:4 promises, "Delight yourself in the Lord, and He will give you the desires of your heart." Make Psalm 63:3 your marriage mission: "My lips will praise you" (ESV). Praise God. Praise each other. And your marriage will forever thrive.

TAKE ACTION

- Have a mindset to have praise continually on your lips. Practice praising God daily as well as praising each other. Here are 10 verses of the many hundreds in the Bible on praising God: Psalm 75:1; 1 Chronicles 16:28; Daniel 2:20; Jeremiah 20:13; Ephesians 1:6; Deuteronomy 10:2; 1 Kings 8:56; Exodus 15:2; Isaiah 63:7; 1 Peter 4:11.

PRAY

Together:

- Use the above scriptures as your praise prayers toward God. Then praise God for your marriage and each other.

TAKING THE NEXT STEP

The heartfelt counsel of a friend is as sweet as perfume and incense.
— Proverbs 27:9

As we discussed at the beginning of this book, seeking good counsel is a sign of wise strength (page 12). Now that you're near the end of this book, I would like to challenge you to take the next step. If you've gone through the majority of these daily devotionals, then you have spent considerable time and energy in acquiring marital wisdom. What would be the best way to retain everything you've learned? I believe it would be by giving it away to other couples. Not necessarily only giving away this book, but by your attained wisdom through godly counsel.

You don't need to have a Ph.D. in psychology or a D.Min. in theology to help others. You shouldn't feel inadequate of your abilities. God has entrusted you with the Holy Spirit to further His kingdom. In his book, *Follow the Cloud*, John Stickl shows the power you have:

- You have been made in God's image and likeness (Gen. 1:26).
- You have everything you need through His divine power (2 Pet. 1:3)
- You have been empowered with His authority (Matt. 28:18–20).
- You have the Spirit of the living God within you (Acts 1:8).
- You are the head and not the tail (Deut. 28:13).
- You are an influencer, not the influenced (Matt. 5:13–14).

This is just a portion of your redemptive potential. In Jesus, you have the potential to:

- create
- build
- inspire
- heal
- restore
- speak life
- release hope
- influence
- and lead!

> That potential is released with every "next step" you take. When you follow God, you become a leader in this world, making the invisible visible, bringing His kingdom into the here and now. Good leaders are simply great followers, and that is your destiny.*

A husband and wife serving together to help others is a powerful force. If you are as disgusted as I am about the rising divorce rate and crumbling, unhappy marriages, then step up and shine the light you have within you. You'll be amazed at how giving godly, heartfelt counsel to others even helps you grow stronger toward a maximum marriage. It's as sweet as perfume and incense!

Perhaps you will forget tomorrow the kind words you say today, but the recipient may cherish them over a lifetime.
— Dale Carnegie

The words of a wise man's mouth are gracious....
— Ecclesiastes 10:12 (AMP)

The godly give good advice to their friends....
— Proverbs 12:26

TAKE ACTION

- Take the "next step" and serve together in a marriage ministry at your church.

PRAY

Him: • Ask God to give you motivation to step up, step out, and step forward in faith in assisting others.

Her: • Thank God for your potential through Jesus.
• Ask God to give you the strength to take a step of faith by reaching out to those in need of marriage help.

**Follow the Cloud,* copyright © 2017 by John Stickl. Published in the United States by Multnomah, an imprint of the Crown Publishing Group, a division of Penguin Random House LLC, New York.

☐☐ GUIDING TO STAY ON TRACK

Where there is no [wise, intelligent] guidance, the people fall [and go off course like a ship without a helm], But in the abundance of [wise and godly] counselors there is victory.

— Proverbs 11:14 (AMP) (See also Proverbs 15:22)

If you have gotten anything from this study of Proverbs, I hope you remember the importance of using kind words (see Kind Words Satisfy, pages 54–57). Kind words:

- are helpful (Prov. 10:32)
- bring healing (Prov. 12:18)
- cheer others up (Prov. 12:25)
- can deflect anger (Prov. 15:1)
- can bring life (Prov. 15:4)
- are persuasive (Prov. 16:23)
- are like honey (Prov. 16:24)
- are like perfume and incense (Prov. 27:9)

What you say probably affects more people than any other action you take. If you've been practicing speaking kindly to your spouse at all times, now would be a good time to spread that kindness to others.

Don't be concerned for your own good but for the good of others.

— 1 Corinthians 10:24

Take the words of Paul to heart in Romans 15:1–4:

> [1]We who are strong must be considerate of those who are sensitive about things like this. We must not just please ourselves. [2]**We should help others do what is right and build them up in the Lord.** [3]For even Christ didn't live to please himself. As the Scriptures say, "The insults of those who insult you, O God, have fallen on me." [4]Such things were written in the Scriptures long ago to teach us. And the Scriptures give us hope and encouragement as we wait patiently for God's promises to be fulfilled.

Then, some of the last words Paul ever wrote were to Timothy challenging him to pass on the wisdom he had gained in life (2 Timothy 3:14–4:2):

> [14]You must remain faithful to the things you have been taught. You know they are true, for you know you can trust those who taught you. [15]You have been taught the holy Scriptures from childhood, and they have given you the wisdom to receive the salvation that comes by trusting in Christ Jesus. [16]All Scripture is inspired by God and is useful to teach us what is true and to make us realize what is wrong in our lives. It corrects us when we are wrong and teaches us to do what is right. [17]God uses it to prepare and equip his people to do every good work.
>
> **[4:1]I solemnly urge you... [2]be prepared, ...patiently correct, rebuke, and encourage people with good teaching.**

People fall and get off track easily in this world because of the power of Satan. But because you have sought out biblical wisdom for your marriage, "you have the power to shape people's thinking, bring them through the minefield of their experiences, help them process a multitude of feelings, and assist in bringing them to a better place in life" (Charles Swindoll Study Bible, page 763). How incredibly rewarding to save someone from derailing or getting off course!

"Regardless of where you are in your marriage today, please know *the full purpose* in the effort you have put forth over these past few months will not be completely fulfilled if:

- You choose to stop working at your own marriage, or
- You choose to not pass what you have learned to another couple" (emphasis mine).*

TAKE ACTION

- There is someone who could benefit from words you can share. Your life experiences have a purpose to teach others. Pray about mentoring other couples.

---

*Taken from *Devoted: God's Design for Marriage*, Copyright © 2016 by Dewey Wilson, Ph.D., Strong Marriages.

PASSING IT ON

Anything you say to the wise will make them wiser. Whatever you tell the righteous will add to their knowledge.

— Proverbs 9:9 (GNT)

Solomon repeats in Proverbs 12:15 and 19:20 the "wise seek counsel." If you have gained a listening ear of someone seeking what you've learned from Scripture, you have been given a opportunity to make this smart person smarter.

If you have a consistent, growing relationship with God, you are qualified to offer Biblical counsel. If you love Christ and genuinely care about the needs of others (see Gal. 6:2), you can guide others. And as you learned with the previous devotional, you are actually called to counsel others.

Let us think of ways to motivate one another to acts of love and good works.

— Hebrews 10:24

Your marriage is your ministry to further the kingdom of God. If you have children, your role is to show them what a Christ-centered marriage looks like. The best way for future generations to learn God's design for marriage is through Christian parents who pass biblical principles to their children.

The Lord says, "I will guide you along the best pathway for your life. I will advise you and watch over you."

— Psalm 32:8

A maximum marriage is a Titus 2 couple and Proverbs 31 couple (pages 220–221). They encourage and counsel others how to live according to God's Word. Research shows that giving of yourself creates happiness. When you give value to others as a couple, it increases your relational "happiness meter" as well.

...Teach what accords with sound doctrine. [2]Older men are to be sober-minded, dignified, self-controlled, sound in faith, in love, and in steadfastness. [3]Older women likewise are to be reverent in behavior, not slanderers or slaves to much wine. They are to teach what is good, [4]and so train the young women to love their husbands and children, [5]to be self-controlled, pure, working at home, kind, and submissive to their own husbands, that the word of God may not be reviled. [10]...so that in everything they may adorn the doctrine of God our Savior.

— Titus 2:1–5; 10 (ESV)

One of the best ideas I ever heard was at a wedding shower being thrown for a young couple about to be married. The host had invited couples who had been married for many years to attend the shower. The young, nearly-wed couple could ask any question, any married advice they wanted, of the older couples. That's great marital counseling!

Keep studying God's Word. Keep making the effort to invest in your relationship with each other. And then pass your knowledge on. A maximum marriage will be yours!

TAKE ACTION

- Be a Titus 2 couple.
- A good resource to have in your library is *Counseling Through Your Bible Handbook* by June Hunt. It provides practical help from Scripture for 50 everyday problems in counseling others.
- Take heed of the following advice from Paul paraphrased magnificently in *The Message:*

Keep your eyes open, hold tight to your convictions, give it all you've got, be resolute, and love without stopping.

— 1 Corinthians 16:13–14 (MSG)

Thank you for using this study for the enrichment of your marriage! Now would be a good time to select a life verse together that portrays your personal marriage vision. It can be a favorite verse or one that you believe to be specifically representative or predictive of your relationship with God and each other. Memorize it. Frame it. Engrave it. Here are a few suggestions:

- Joshua 1:9
- Psalm 37:4
- Proverbs 3:5–6
- Proverbs 24:3-4
- Ecclesiastes 4:12
- Isaiah 40:31
- Jeremiah 17:7–8
- Jeremiah 29:11
- Mark 10:9
- Romans 8:28
- Romans 12:10
- Romans 15:5-6
- 1 Corinthians 13:7
- Ephesians 4:2–3
- Ephesians 4:32
- Ephesians 5:2
- Galatians 5:22-23
- Philippians 4:6-7
- Colossians 3:14
- Hebrews 10:23
- 1 Peter 4:8
- 1 John 4:7
- 1 John 4:19

My prayer is that you have a prosperous, joyful, life-long, maximum marriage.

"May the LORD bless you and protect you.
May the LORD smile on you and be gracious to you.
May the LORD show you his favor and give you his peace."
— Numbers 6:24-26